D0143561

THE AUDACITY
OF RACES AND GENDERS

THE AUDACITY
OF RACES AND GENDERS

A personal and global story
of the Obama election

ZILLAH EISENSTEIN

Zed Books
LONDON & NEW YORK

The Audacity of Races and Genders: A personal and global story of the Obama election was first published in 2009 by Zed Books Ltd, 7 Cynthia Street, London N1 9JF, UK and Room 400, 175 Fifth Avenue, New York, NY 10010, USA

www.zedbooks.co.uk

FSC
Mixed Sources
Product group from well-managed
forests and other controlled sources
Cert no. SGS-COC-2953
www.fsc.org
© 1996 Forest Stewardship Council

Typeset in Sabon by Long House Publishing Services
Index by John Barker
Cover design by Alice Marwick
Printed and bound in Great Britain by CPI Antony Rowe, Chippenham and Eastbourne

Distributed in the USA exclusively by Palgrave Macmillan, a division of St Martin's Press, LLC, 175 Fifth Avenue, New York, NY 10010, USA

A catalogue record for this book is available from the British Library
Library of Congress Cataloging in Publication Data is available

ISBN 978 1 84813 419 5 hb
ISBN 978 1 84813 420 1 pb
ISBN 978 1 84813 421 8 eb

Contents

... for all my "intimate others"
who turn my heart towards the sky

Acknowledgements

This book is a somewhat untraditional project for me. The writing of it has pulled on such personally intimate connections and relationships to my political self that simple acknowledgements will not do. I instead need to give thanks.

My mind, along with my body, is written here. So my heart is also easily found. I thank all of my friends, especially my intimate others; my colleagues; my doctors; my sports buddies; my yoga teachers; my family; and my students. And as with the narrative that emerges here, these grouped identities are, more often than not, porous and permeable rather than distinct from each.

Most of the ideas found here have been a part of my thinking and writing and living for the past thirty-plus years. So whatever is new in these pages is also not wholly new. I have simply continued to work and rework my thoughts alongside and with new historical and cultural and economic developments. Please engage my earlier books in order to see the careful documentation and recognition of the many ideas that I am deeply indebted to in these pages.

My ideas and thoughts, as always, continue to meander, and change, and shift in dialogue with my amazing coterie of friends and colleagues and in political activism throughout the US and across the globe. My thinking and writing are fully indebted to these people's generous intellect. I am truly blessed to have had so many of these people on this present journey with me. Some of the people have been with me from the start of my writing career. Others have participated more intermittently. Others are new to my work with the Obama campaign.

Thank you to Miriam Brody who has read every word I have ever written, starting at my beginning. Her thoughtful insights are embedded in my words. Thank you to Patty Zimmermann, Rosalind Petchesky, Susan Buck-Morss, Carla Golden, Chandra Mohanty, bell hooks, Mary Katzenstein, Anna Marie Smith, Thomas Shevory and Richard Stumbar who have read large portions of the book. Patty and Susan read the entirety; Patty helped clarify my phrasing, while Susan cheered on my optimism and helped with the subtitle. Everyone's criticisms, and queries, and curiosity pushed me to discover what I was trying to say. Thanks to Naeem Inayatalluh, Asma Barlas, and Peyi Airewele Soyinka for helping me wonder if I have thought widely and broadly enough. The conversations with Angela Davis, Beverly Guy-Sheftall, Hamid Dabashi, Golbarg Bashi, Patricia McFadden, and Linda Carty have enriched my insights to new and needed depths. My discussions with Bernadette Muthien always keep me thinking about South Africa. Maud Edwards and Judith Astelerra remind me of the incredible changes in Sweden and Spain. My friends Donald Dowsland, Joan Sara Romm and Janet Haskell have graciously and continuously supplied me with a responsive ear. Women activists in Iran, Rwanda, India, Korea, Sudan, Iraq, Pakistan and Afghanistan continue to expand my understanding of gender's many meanings.

Much of the writing found here was readily circulated and distributed by www.CommonDreams.org, by the Association for Women's Rights in Development at www.awid.org, and by Aishah Shahidah Simmons at www.afrolezproductions.com. Salah Hassan of Cornell University's Africana Center generously posted my writings on list serves throughout the continent of Africa. Early versions of the writings on Hillary Clinton traveled widely on the web and were translated into Polish, Spanish, Chinese, Japanese, Serbo-Croat, French, and so on. The enormously supportive responses that I received to the writing greatly encouraged me with this project. African American women's generous support of "Hillary is White" allowed me continuous opportunity for rich and complex dialogue with which to grow.

I met many people along the way working in the Obama campaign that enriched my belief in political possibilities. Several of them have become cherished friends. Tracy Kemble, Karen Andre, Carol Boyce Davies, Johnetta Cole, Mary Laraia, dc McGuire, and all the phone bankers in the Liberty City office, thank you.

Thanks as well to all the people I spent time with in Sweden, South Africa, Paris, South Korea, and on the rest of my travels where I shared my thoughts about the Obama campaign.

My special thanks to Rebecca Riley, my (almost) lifelong friend who pulled me into the campaign, as you will read. We canvassed together in Philadelphia and Miami. Ellen Wade, my intimate other since graduate school days and our work in the women's movement, was right by my side as I forayed into electoral activism.

My doctors Adam Law, Charles Garbo, and Sami Husseini in Ithaca, New York, made it possible for me to never be totally defined by the limits of medicine. Doctors Bernie Bochner and Dennis Chi at Sloane Kettering took their expertise and fought for me with it. Victoria Wood always made sure I had the latest nutritional assist.

Friends at Island Health Club—Barb and Terry Ciaschi, Kelly Chase, Huldah Boruchovitz, Leo Muzzy and Bill and Cheri Farell cheered me throughout my chemo regime. Barb always was ready to hear my latest thought about race, or gender, or Obama.

Thanks to Jim Best for getting me the latest books with no time to do so. A special thanks to Judy Dietz, for her assist in the last stages of preparing the manuscript.

I feel very privileged to have been able to work, once again, with Zed Books in the publication of this book. My editor Tamsine O'Riordan made helpful suggestions to make the book more accessible. Jakob Horstmann was wonderfully generous with his time as Production Assistant. Alice Marwick designed a fabulous cover. Pat Harper, for a third time, copy-edited my book and made sense of my peculiar use of words.

My sister Julia Eisenstein remains my lifeline after too much family loss.

P. K. Das and Tilu Bal Das, who correspond often from Mumbai, remind me just how large my life is.

My nephew Michael Eisenstein helps remind me of my optimism.

My daughter Sarah Eisenstein Stumbar buoys my spirit each and every day and is why I have such hope.

My spouse Richard Stumbar is my rock and helps me live each day as though it is a life.

Introducing
My Mindscape

1

Fluid Frames

I have chosen a method of writing that allows me the openness and momentariness and changeability that I need in order to think "newly". Thinking "newly" means seeing what was not evident or seeable before, seeing what was formerly unknown, seeing what might happen next. So thoughts meander as they need to and should; are concluded and then reappear; are exposed and then become shadows and whispers. My mind's wanderings and meanderings began early on when Barack Obama declared his candidacy for president of the United States. I wondered if there was a formerly unknowable kind of politics emerging: a new set of political possibilities to discover and find. And my wondering continues to this day.

As such, this book is random[1] and unpredictable, but only in the way that life itself is so. The way one person survives the massacre in Mumbai, and another dies. The way one sister is born with a genetic mutation, and another is not. Often it is simple curiosity that leads me one place rather than another. I sometimes write in diary form in order to expose the variability of my thinking. Instead of creating an enforced coherence, I show the back and forth of my political thoughts as they emerge. The story narrated here has no clarifying beginning because each present moment is already connected to previous histories and realignments. My earlier books also map the journey I have taken to establish the many ongoing dialogues found in these next pages.

The inside story of this book—an unconventional storytelling of the 2008 US presidential election—has just begun. The outside story—written with added context of the economic and military crises of the globe—unfolds daily. Media-ted election noise drowns out the complexities and multi-vocal viewpoints of both inside and outside, often creating a global monologue, rather than the needed multiple dialogues.

I describe leafleting in the north side of Philadelphia, in predominantly black and poor neighborhoods during the primaries, and I end in Liberty City, Florida, helping to get out the early vote the week before the election. I share ongoing discussions with friends and colleagues in the US who speak with their various identities—Pakistani, Iranian, Ghanaian and so on—and with friends and activists on my visits to South Africa, Spain, France and Sweden. While interrogating the anti-Islamic narrations at home and abroad, I ask people in the US to listen to Chinua Achebe's guidance. Gay marriage, gender bending, Turkish and Iranian feminisms, new notions of the secular/religious divide, the Chinese Olympics, and the global economic crash, are threaded and webbed together in idiosyncratic fashion.

I reconfigure and reframe the complex engendered and racialized historical trajectory of Obama's victory. The 25 different frames, or chapters, presented here form an unlikely porous grid through which to examine the economic excesses of capitalism at present while the price of oil ebbs and flows, and the price of food skyrockets across the globe. Each frame seeks to expose the particular way that sex, race and class interweave with and without regard to nation.

Meanwhile, the rest of the world watched the US 2008 election thinking they should have a right to vote given that they will live by the new rules, or lack of them, that the next administration puts in play. But the election is part of the embedded systems of power and cannot be understood without its global context, as nations and their "patriotism" pretend they are self-contained within their own borders.

A key thematic of this book is that sex, heteronormative gender, and race—specifically its white privilege—in their specific class definition are historically routed/rooted constructs and are more fluid than they are static. There are cross-cultural vectors of contact that both statically encrust and also reframe and change them. So politics and political possibility remain in flux with the shifting meanings and new constructions of race and gender. Because the racializing of gender and the engendering of race are in continual process it is not always easy or possible to know the truthfulness of these categories. It is why gender and race can pose in decoy fashion: a female body that does not believe in women's rights, or a black person who denies the significance of race. In this fashion, misogyny and white privilege are continually formulated through newly strange locations and configurations.

Global flows of labor are changing gender and racial constructions; the newest militarism of the US also does so. As these structural needs of power change, gender and with it its white privilege morphs. The 2008 primaries tell this story as it is written with and on the bodies of Hillary Clinton and Barack and Michelle Obama. New racial formations both subvert earlier forms, and reinscribe them with established heteronormative gendered meanings. Yet the newest constructions of race and gender and their class realignments also chart unknowable new trajectories.

The effects are hardly linear. Progressive possibilities emerge alongside possibilities that are incredibly anti-democratic. White privilege and gender are not static biological constructions, so they shift and change with class formations. Therefore, I am always looking for their newest formulations and intersections. As race and gender often expose their own malleability and fluidity they undermine the normalizing of biological gender and race. So it was pretty clear to many that Sarah Palin was being used as a decoy of sorts; one vagina is not necessarily exchangeable with another, even though Sarah was offered up as an alternative to Hillary.

Although gender and racial white privilege change they also are unchanging, or in part stagnant. These categories often reproduce themselves without a newly clear articulation and then frame our thoughts in outmoded ways. Patriarchy, misogyny, and their racialized forms morph and don't. So Michelle is mommie-in-chief, but not quite like Laura Bush. Obama, a "new" man of sorts, is still the one who is president, not Michelle. Hillary eventually becomes Secretary of State while Bill angles for center stage, to not look wifely. The world is black, and brown, and yellow so Barack looks like more of the world than he does not. He is a perfect choice for the multi-colored globe while Clinton stands in for the newly complex notions of gender, looking somewhat "yesterday". Women are elected as presidents in Liberia, and Chile, and Germany, and Argentina despite the glass ceiling in the US.

I must continually open the newest ways of thinking, what I term the "newly new" in order to see and to find insights that are not readily available. I use the awkward phrase "newest-new" or "newly new" to call attention to the way that what we think of as new, is often not in its newest form because it is changing and becoming newer still. New is not a stagnant category. New is always in process. So there is new, and newer and newest; and yet this process always weaves the old along with the present. In this sense, the new or newest is never simply that because it is *also* "new-old" simultaneously.[2] The "before", which is in some sense old, remains a part of this process.

My focus in these following frames is to open myself and my readers to what is new and maybe unknown in order to build new political possibilities. That which is new represents change, and often feels uncomfortable because it is not necessarily easily known. The familiar, the knowable, is often thought to be more comforting. I ask you to travel with me, embracing the discomfort.

I therefore always want to be looking for what has changed and is changing, and the new capacities that are to be found in this process. Some will think that I see too much as new; others will think I do not see enough of what has changed. I see old in the newly new, a togetherness of sorts. My sense of an undetermined and unknown set of political possibilities emanates from here.

I am an activist and political theorist who has critiqued elections as superstructure and symbolic rather than structural and real. I never expected to write and decipher election talk. To choose this inside location was new for me. Because the storytelling from inside loses the needed critical lens, I position the election always with an outside, and I keep changing the location of the outside. But it is also hard to keep the borders clear between them because the borders are porous and permeable. Maybe this is why people choose to locate themselves in one place or the other, rather than in both. So radicals of all sorts who dismissed Obama from the start felt too outside to me; and people who thought that he was the new Messiah felt too inside.

Obama's presidency has pledged to bring about change—to fix the problems that keep the US from its promissory for all. Yet Obama offers himself as proof of the possibility of success. "We" the people, need change; and the Obamas are proof that change can happen. They were born black and poor and they now occupy the White House. Dreams can come true. This is a delicate and dangerous storyline.

I remember watching the first night of the Democratic convention, in August 2008, and afterwards feeling as though maybe I had made a mistake to get so involved in the campaign. The Obama family looked too picturebook beautiful, too perfect, too color-coordinated, too American Dream for me. Although the successes of Barack and Michelle are proof of the change that can happen in America they also prove that much more change is needed for their story to become anybody's let alone everyone's. Yet, the next morning when I awoke I was back in the fold. It felt miraculous that a black family stood in for everyone's dreams.

On election day, November 4, 2008, Barack Obama was the only plausible alternative to the present language of colonization that defines too much of humanity as *un*employed, *un*documented, *il*legal, and *un*healthy.[3] These were desperate times. The fascistic militarist direction of the Bush regime must be formidably redirected, most especially in Iraq and Afghanistan. Whether and how Obama will take this path remains to be seen.

As I write it is not clear how this story, or my story, will end — what new formations US empire will take and whether it will embrace, or be forced to embrace, a more democratic dialogue and relationship with the globe. Nevertheless, the 2008 election is a beginning toward launching a serious challenge to neo-liberalism and global capitalism's newest forms of hetero-normative militarized racialized gender and sexualized racism. Leaders — in Britain, Poland, and Australia — who were aligned with Bush/Cheney and their war in Iraq lost public support.

I hope we will want Obama to stay for a second term. But, if not, there is a better starting point for the next time and the next struggle than there was with Bush/Cheney. I am hoping for new, even if small, beginnings that will matter greatly.

Notes

1   I do not mean random in the popular cyber gaming usage.
2   See my *Global Obscenities, Patriarchy, Capitalism and the Lure of Cyberfantasy* (New York: New York University Press, 1998), for a discussion of my early use and depiction of the concept 'new-old'.
3   Linda Tuhiwai Smith, *Decolonizing Methodologies* (London: Zed Books, 1999), pp. 26, 27.

2

Bodies and Me
. . . .

I think and meander with my body. It is forever present even when it is not being mentioned. "Bodies have memories" even when we try to silence or deny them.[1] Bodies also always wear their sex and color and storylines so they are very much a part of the political narrative told here.

Obama is slender, and agile, and looks very young. He moves with "physical grace ... like an athlete much more than a politician, taking pleasure in his body" as he bounds onto the stage with total energy. And his hands are always clapping, while his arms reach outwards to the crowds. McCain's body told a very different story. He moved slowly and stiffly. His "prolonged suffering" as a prisoner of war has ruined his shoulders so he cannot raise his arms and physically embrace his followers by doing so. Instead he appeared distant, and hobbled.[2]

Our bodies are also lenses into the randomness of life. We do not choose our bodies. They choose us. And, when they fall seriously ill they can take over and demand too much. I started writing this book while I was still recovering from invasive cancer surgery, and on chemotherapy. Because I cannot be sure exactly how my struggle with cancer has impacted my thinking, it is a story to reveal. It is just now about a year since the treatments ended and I feel more myself again. Yet I look at my scar-marked body with its closed wounds and remember, but not fully.[3] My scars "expose the injury" and remind me of my bodily emotions, as Sara Ahmed might say.[4]

The following details are not important, and yet set the stage. One day in the early part of April 2007 I saw a bit of blood in my urine. I had just come in from my usual run, and felt fine, so I pushed back at my thoughts and hoped the blood would not appear again. I continued daily life: running, doing my yoga, doing Nautilus weights, teaching my classes, living contentedly. I left for a conference in Paris forgetting about the blood. I had breast cancer many years ago and prophylactic surgeries to protect me from my risk of further breast or ovarian cancer so I simply hoped the blood was an aberration, or maybe a kidney stone, or something else easier than cancer. My daughter Sarah was studying for the Medical College Admission Test in order to apply to medical school in the fall and I just could not let myself consider that I was in jeopardy. So I didn't, although I also did.

Upon my return from Paris, and after a long hard run to assuage my jet lag, my urine had turned to all blood. My friend and doctor Sami Husseini found what he thought at first was a bladder tumor, but the surgery revealed a much more complicated challenge. Miriam and Isaac and Biddy and Peggy made hurried phone calls to get me to the best specialists. I went with my partner Richard to Sloane Kettering for further diagnosis that kept changing: from the rare urachal cancer—the urachus is an embryonic remnant—to a peritoneal ovarian-like cancer, back to the possibility that it was bladder cancer.

The complexity of the tumor defied easy identity. Doctors Chi and Bochner nonetheless removed the tumor and part of my bladder with great skill and precision. Numerous biopsies were done and found benign. Although I appeared "clean" the tumor board at Sloane-Kettering pressed me hard to do chemotherapy treatments because of the unknown status of the tumor. Sarah asked me to do the chemo because she could not bear that if I died without doing the treatments, she would wonder each and every day for the rest of her life if I might have lived. So we—my wonderfully large number of intimate friends and family—would begin chemo.

I was told at the start that the cancer was rare and aggressive and life-threatening. Somehow I suppressed the grief and simply disallowed it. I remember not crying. I was calm and peaceful because I just so fiercely wanted to be. I knew I was at the edge of something, even if I could not know exactly what this edge was. I did not want the cancer to dominate me.

I desperately wanted to face into the cancer celebrating my life while looking at death. I kept thinking that maybe if I could face dying, I could face living without being able to know if I would live. I was trying to blend and blur the lines of living and dying. I felt defiant and exhausted at the same time. I would fight for my life while accepting death if it came. I kept reminding myself that I had loved my life, and that brought deep, deep solace. So I felt affirmative, hopeful that I could make something of this random assault. I was profoundly sad, but not desperate.

I needed to accept the possibility of death so that I would know if and when to stop trying to live. Yet, as Zadie Smith writes of her dad's dying, "death doesn't happen at all … it is, in fact, the opposite of a happening"; that "facing death's absurd non-face" is the only choice. She reminds us that death "cannot be conquered, defied, contemplated, or even approached, because it's not there; it's only a word, signifying nothing". The death of funerals, the death we mark, "is a fake".[5] But I was not thinking about the fake. I was looking to know and accept that there is an end. That Sarah would have to and could live on, without me.

I did not want to deny death as a necessary truth, at the same time that I wanted to live, if I could. I wanted to live with an acceptance of my mortality, unlike how Susan Sontag's son, David Rieff, describes his mother's death, as "unreconciled to mortality, even after suffering so much pain". He was in agony wishing that she could let go, could not "love life so much".[6] She would only speak of her survival, never her death. And years after her death he agonizes that he did not do enough. I knew I did not want this for Sarah, or Richard, or any of my intimate circle.

I talked about dying to help prepare myself and Richard and Sarah and my sister Julia and my other intimates in case I did. I made myself think of the cancer as a part of me, rather than as an enemy. I began to move through to some other place. Sarah and Richard reassured me that they could help me do everything I would have to do. Without my beloved, remarkable, boundless coterie of friends I would not have done any of this. I would just have closed my eyes.

The recovery from the surgery was almost impossible. I think my body thought the healing spasms were beyond doable. The searing pain was unrelenting and engulfed every part of me, first for days and then for weeks. I used few pain drugs because they disallowed any kind of semblance of life. I missed eating. I missed thinking that it was not cancer. I missed regular, ordinary, wonderful life.

My body slowly healed. The scars knitted. The twitching stopped. The shooting pains subsided. I painstakingly moved toward quietude and gained strength. There was an absence of pain. There were daily visits from my cherished friends bringing flowers, and scarves, and easily digestible foods, and quiet sittings. There was the constant stream of cards and letters. There was immense love.

I started taking halting walks to the end of our street. Life was slowly beginning again. Then, too soon, chemo started and it pulled at me and scratched its way into my peace. But I pushed back as hard as I could. I began to take my runs again but with my feet lower to the ground. I pulled my heart towards the sky in yoga with renewed hope. I was fragile, and also not. I was getting through and beyond all this hardship.

But my body's story is not my own to tell. The deep love of my extraordinary friends and my family made my body theirs as well. My body's energy was rediscovered with their energy. My body's determination was sustained by their determination. My willingness to live was their expectation that I must. My pain did not leave me alone or lonely although it was "solitary". It was a shared pain that connected me to powerful resources of compassion and comfort as my loved ones "bore witness" for me.[7]

My doctors in Ithaca—Sami and Charles and Adam—were completely present with their brilliance and their love. Doctors

Chi and Bochner along with the nurses at Sloane mobilized my spirit by their sheer commitment to the living. Debbie in the recovery room continuously wet my lips, never taking a minute for herself and giving impeccable care. Betty Ramos emptied my drains while always smiling at me even though she drove one and a half hours each way to work and had a young son waiting for her at home. Hard-working medical residents scuttled in and out of my room worrying that there might be something else they could do.

I am completely fortunate to have good health insurance from my place of work. I know the US medical system is wrecked and broken but my treatment stood in defiance of this. Each of my doctors was completely committed and gifted. Every one of the aides and nurses assisting me were overworked and underpaid and yet they forged ahead with total tenderness. We started out as strangers to each other and yet they filled me with caring and love. The people and friends who surrounded me were ferocious with their empathy and energy.

This unbelievable generous caring—from intimate beloved friends as well as from strangers—makes me deeply believe in the wonder of the everyday kind of people. This belief in people's love is the energy that fueled my recovery, and my hope that we, everyday and ordinary people, can make a better world.

Sarah was finishing her semester at Columbia's School of Public Health. She would come daily to Sloane-Kettering and help me walk the hallways with all my tubes. Richard and Ellen and Rebecca kept a twenty-four-hour vigil while I slowly moved through the early post-surgical days in the hospital. Susan and Eric lent their apartment to Richard so he could have easy access to the hospital. Chandra came to New York City to help Richard bring me home to Ithaca. I couldn't imagine the travel with all the jostling to my body, but it was done.

Back in Ithaca, Miriam had cooked chicken soup and prepared jello—of all things—for my compromised digestive tract. They were in the kitchen when we arrived. Carla lovingly prepared protein drinks in the hopes I would put on a few pounds and find energy. Satya made yogurt from scratch. Asma cooked bland Pakistani food instead of her usual spicy dishes. Judy and Jerry Dietz kept delivering homemade sweets. Patty lectured for me at school every fifth Tuesday during chemo when I could not stand erect. She and Anna Marie filled the freezer with spinach and potato soups. Mary and Peter made muffins and brought flowers from the farmers' market. Elizabeth and Betsy had dinners delivered regularly.

Donald came and lay on my bed just so I could feel his presence. And before chemo he shaved my head and cried. Janet made a vast array of elegant hats for me in every color and weave. Joan decorated my body with beautiful clothes. Julia took over the total care of our mother Fannie suffering Alzheimer's so she would be spared knowing about my cancer. Victoria oversaw a regime of nutrient supplements to help me heal. Suzanne and Tai, and Rebecca, and Leah wrote letters reminding me of how rich life is. Toni kept the house beautiful and calm. Lanessa gently realigned my body in yoga class. Tilu and P. K. traveled from Mumbai to reassure me that they were not too far away.

I received and accepted prayers from Christians, Jews, Muslims, Hindus, and atheists. It truly takes a very very big village ...

These extraordinary, beloved people in my life became my spirit when I had little of my own. I was enmeshed in their glorious generosity when my compromised singular self was not enough. Their intimate presence in my being made me more than myself, when I could not face ahead singularly. They created a community of the deepest forms of affection, embrace, support, and generosity of heart. They pulled me toward life in the face of death. They turned the horrifying words—an aggressive cancer—into something liveable. I love the world that they allow me to believe in.

Uncannily I happened to read Rosi Braidotti just after writing these thoughts. She writes of an "ethics of affirmation" which recognizes "pain as transformative" when people connect deeply and affirmatively, rather than passively, in order to move beyond grief and trauma. She compels us to move through our sense of sadness and mourning to a defiant resistance. She celebrates "a ritual of bonding and rebirth". I so agree with her when she concludes: "We have to grow worthy of everything that happens to us."[8] And we do not do this alone.

Amazing love assured me of the possibilities of human connectivity. My friends pulled me toward them with their uncompromising devotion. In this busy and harried world, no one was too busy. And because the very personal is very political I became fully aware of why I so deeply believe in the necessity and possibility of improving the world we inhabit. Extraordinary ordinary people make social justice alluring. My struggle with cancer allows me "a micro universalist claim"[9] that hopeful possibilities of a shared and interconnected defiance and subversion promise the possibility of a transformative politics.

And then the 2008 presidential primaries got very nasty. All my thinking and writing about race and gender for these many years was now center and front in the electoral arena. Feminism was pitted against civil rights; Hillary spoke on behalf of gender and Barack was labeled black. It was all too reminiscent of a troublesome past that heartbreakingly split the connections between race and gender, especially for my beloved African American women friends. I wanted to use my personal hopefulness to impact this troubled political moment.

Maybe living is simply an act of hope to begin with—that the imprint we make with our life will matter enough to make the struggle worth it. Maybe this is why I turned on my computer to start writing again when I did, beginning to believe that everyday ordinary people *might* help Obama change the face of empire. I was a bit wobbly, and my bald head was wrapped in my Nigerian turban, but I was finding my political defiance thanks to my indomitable intimate others.

Months later I read the African Rights report on post-genocide Rwandan justice and was overwhelmed with remembering the physical and psychic pain of Tutsi survivors attempting to redress their mass killings, and torture and rape. I read their harrowing descriptions and kept thinking of their bodies and their scarring.[10] The horrific Israeli bombings of Palestinians in Gaza began December 28, 2008, killing well over one thousand people and maiming thousands more. My cancer is benign in comparison.

Nevertheless I hope. Maybe my own hope that I am healthy and will survive resonates with Barack's talk about hope. Some days I feel triumphant. Other days I do not. I let go of each day as best I can and then grab the next.

Notes

1   Jay Prosser, "Skin Memories", in Sara Ahmed and Jackie Stacey, eds., *Thinking Through the Skin* (New York: Routledge, 2001), p. 52.
2   Mark Danner, "Obama and Sweet Potato Pie", *New York Review of Books*, vol. LV, no. 18 (November 20, 2008), pp. 12, 18.
3   Tina Takemoto, "Open Wounds", in Ahmed and Stacey, eds., *Thinking Through the Skin*, p. 112.
4   Ahmed, *Cultural politics of Emotion* (New York: Routledge, 2004), p. 202.
5   Zadie Smith, "Dead Man Laughing", *New Yorker*, December 22 and 29, 2008), p. 84.
6   David Rieff, *Swimming in a Sea of Death* (New York: Simon & Schuster, 2008), pp. 13, 14.
7   Sara Ahmed, *The Cultural Politics of Emotion*, pp. 21, 29, 31.
8   Rosi Braidotti, "Affirmation, Pain and Empowerment", *Asian Journal of Women's Studies*, vol. 14, no. 3 (2008), pp. 19, 23, 27.
9   Ibid., p. 15.
10 African Rights Working for Justice, "Survivors and Post-Genocide Justice in Rwanda", published by African Rights and Redress, November 2008. Available at www.afrights.org, or www.redress.org.

A New
Circular Globe

....

3

Ch/India and New-Old Economies

Economic crisis, global capital, the price of oil, the cost of food, and the slums inhabited by too many are all part of one interconnected, painful story. This new unfolding story, and Ch/India's place in it, however, also has a history.

US and European domination of the globe is relatively new if one is thinking backwards in history. Until the 1400s, China and India were the largest and most formidable economies on the globe. If one acknowledges this, one might be less likely to be surprised that they are a main economic challenge to the US today despite today's global economic crisis.

The US lost more than 30 million jobs after the 1980s while China and India were creating new labor markets.[1] It is unclear how the global economic crisis will affect China's growing status as it reported in February 2009 that some 20 million of the rural migrant workforce, one in seven, had been laid off. With the economic credit crunch, hundreds of China's toy manufacturing companies have closed.

Yet China's new-old status reminds us to recognize the new while not forgetting the old. It is more often than not the case that established misinformed ways of seeing remain in place and therefore disallow a seeing of the newest-new. So the ignorance that assumes a misguided former history disallows a seeing of the most recent newness along with a continuity of the before.

Neither China nor India is usually given its historical or cultural due by the imperial US. Neither can be richly understood in the present given this imperial ignorance. These two nations today account for one third of the planet's population. Extraordinary amounts of the world's goods for trade are built in China with software and circuitry designed in India. By mid-century China's share of global output is expected to be around 45 percent, while in 2008 it was 6 percent. Ch/India is a major consumer, supplier, competitor, innovator, investor, and source of skilled labor. Even with the latest global economic crisis China still promises to spend approximately $586 billion dollars (that is, roughly 7 percent of its gross domestic product) on infrastructure—on its railways, its subways and its airports.

In spite of the latest economic downturn, exports in China have risen 850 percent since 1990, and China is now arguably the "most competitive manufacturing platform ever". India, on the other hand, is vital in software, design, services, and technical and corporate innovation. Her greatest export is low-cost high-skill services. India contributes upwards of 60 percent of the US economy with the service labor it provides. China predominates in supplying low-cost manufacture and India in high-technology services.[2]

Both countries provide incredibly massive consumer markets as well. China is presently the biggest consumer of cell phones with 350 million subscribers in summer 2008. And the poor of these countries—some four billion strong—are more often viewed in the global market as a growth opportunity than as a burden. It is estimated that by 2025, China will consume 14.2 percent of the world's energy; importing 75 percent of the crude oil it uses. It has begun oil exploration in Australia, Indonesia, Iran, Nigeria, and Sudan, to name a few of its sites.

India imports 73 percent of its oil from the Middle East, at a cost of at least $21 billion a year. The disproportionate costs and global demand will continue to rise even as oil prices dip. As skills rise while China and India graduate more college students than the US the better-paying jobs will move to these countries, and labor will become more expensive as well.[3] The economic locations of power are shifting, and more rapidly than recognized. It is hard to overstate the increasing importance and presence of both China and India on the global scene, even with the unknowns of the present global economic crisis.[4]

This new geopolitics is rooted/routed in the global flows of manufacture and service labor. It charts a changing economic structure of the globe and the changing place of the US within it. These flows take place within and alongside cultural shifts that have people traveling and migrating from their home countries to places that promise opportunity. Migrants continue to flock to the US with much less opportunity awaiting them there. This incredible migration mix was clearly in evidence when the national teams entered the Olympic stadium in Beijing. Nigeria's team was made up of Nigerians, Cuba's of Cubans, and Jamaica's of Jamaicans; the US team was made up of people from all these countries. One wonders how the complexion of the globe will continue to shift as global capital destroys the fabric that has held its promise in the US for this long.

Nevertheless, the newly elected Barack Obama promises a hopeful politics premised on the unique opportunities available in the US. The members of his and Michelle's extended family represent a smattering of the peoples of the globe mixing histories of Kenya, Indonesia, Canada, and the US. "The family that produced Barack and Michelle Obama is black and white and Asian, Christian, Muslim and Jewish. They speak English; Indonesian; French; Cantonese; German; Hebrew; African languages including Swahili, Luo and Igbo; and even a few phrases of Guliah, the Creole dialect of the South Carolina Low-country."[5] This fluidity is the newly new global construction of racial identity that Obama brings to the US presidency.

But the excess of wealth on the one hand, and desperate destitution on the other, continue in outrageous new forms to this day as part of the remains of earlier forms of global capital. One only needs to be reminded of the slave ship, or colonial slave plantations, or colonial effects in India or Algeria, or the imperial exploitation of Chile or South Africa. Many of these earlier forms of excess were more racially homogeneous, more geographically contained, and more singularly defined. Today's exploitation and dehumanization cut through and across races, and with this, gender, in newer, more economically differentiated complex form.

There are very rich blacks in Cape Town alongside the black poverty in the townships. Barack Obama is the first black president, while blacks also remain disproportionately poor and disproportionately incarcerated in US prisons. Such economic diversity did not exist for blacks during South African apartheid or US slavery. Alongside the complexly newly racialized globe there is sometimes also less choice, and more dominion, given the fall of the Soviet Union as a counteralternative. Unilateral and uni-polar rule by the US and transnational capital during the Bush regime has written a newer form of anti-democratic 'terror capitalism' that used more force and more torture, and has denied human rights.

Free markets during Bush's regime were tied to a less free and less democratic politics—a politics of torture and brutality that was also, much like exploitation itself, historically more readily mired in third-world countries. US empire is no stranger to violence, but it was unabashedly newly authorized through a decade of Bush/Cheney rule. First-world countries have depended on and created totalitarian regimes elsewhere before, but today totalitarian democracy is also newly formed. Today the poverty, like the torture, and the third world itself, is more dispersed and less homogeneous. Obama promises to redirect anti-democratic moves and re-establish the rule of law. The rest of the globe, along with many North Americans, have given him their trust that he will do so.

Naomi Klein's writing about how notions of "disaster" and "shock" are used by capitalists to enforce punishing remedies for their own benefit appears incredibly apt for this present moment.[6] Capital is legalizing its exploitative side more and more. While the super-rich in the US can legally protect their incomes, ordinary wage earners' earnings are carefully surveilled. In 2000, the top 400 taxpayers received 1.1 percent of all income in the US, whereas in 1992 they received 0.5 percent. Between 1980 and 2002, 18 million couples filed for bankruptcy—one in eight households. In 1997 the richest 1 percent of Americans had as much to spend after taxes as the bottom 49 million; in 1999 they had as much as the bottom 100 million.[7] These numbers reveal the newest-new excesses of global capital. And this newest form of unregulated and illegal exploitation, originating from the US and its banks, has created an unconscionable economic crisis for the globe. Klein's notion of capital's "shock doctrine" has gone worldwide.

The economic excess continues and it necessitates less equality and less freedom as well. The transnational oil companies reap their profits no matter what the price of oil is. Their excessive wealth is way beyond the everyday imagination. Chevron made $14 billion in 2005, and in the first quarter of 2006 they were well on their way to making $28 billion. Meanwhile, Bush's militarist neoliberal agenda allowed for and protected the search for gas and oil wherever it might lead.

The price of oil was pretty steady—approximately $3 a barrel until 1973 when prices increased greatly in the so-called "oil crisis" of that year. Next the price of oil went close to $12 a barrel. More recently, in early 2008, oil sold at more than $100 a barrel with the expectation that demand would continue to rise at least 2 percent a year. By early 2009 the price of a barrel of oil had plunged and was fluctuating between $40 and $70 a barrel. In this age of energy imperialism the geopolitics of oil sets the standard for environmental and political degradation.[8] Wars are fought to protect greed—wars in Afghanistan, and Iraq, and Sudan, and wherever oil is to be found.

The globe is also now faced with a dire food crisis. Of the more than 6 billion people on the earth today, almost 1 billion live in a state of chronic hunger. The cost of food soars, while fuel costs fluctuate. In spite of this food crisis, more emphasis is being placed on growing crops such as soybeans and corn which can be used for fuel than on feeding people. The production of biofuels—ethanol or palm oil—is at direct odds with the need to feed people. China and India are both turning toward more importation of food and fuel which only creates more global havoc over prices and accessibility.[9] By the year 2030 it is expected that there will be 8.3 billion people on Earth and that farmers will need to grow 30 percent more grain in order to feed them. Yet soil degradation along with a skewed set of food and oil prices only make this task all the more daunting.

According to Mike Davis the present globe is a "planet of slums", not cities; poverty, not opportunity; unemployment, not jobs; despair, not hope. These slums have no "traditional cores" or "recognizable peripheries"; instead, urban characteristics exist in rural areas, and urban areas have rural character. Since the 1970s more than 200 million Chinese have moved from rural to urban areas. And today more than 80 percent of Marx's industrial proletariat is now living in China or somewhere outside of Western Europe and the US. People cram the cities not because of the supply of jobs but because they have nowhere else to go.

This extreme poverty and lack of alternatives is why rapid urbanization produces slums, and not cities. Through the 1980s up to 90 percent of urban household growth took place in slums. Indian slums grew 250 percent faster than the overall population.[10] If this trend continues the urban world will be one of squalor, and future cities will be made not of glass and steel but of scrap wood. As early as 2015, black Africa will have 332 million slum dwellers; this population is expected to double every fifteen years.[11]

Davis posits that globally the numbers of slum dwellers and the urban poor could reach 2 billion people—50 percent of city dwellers by 2040. In the poorest nations almost one third of the global population already live in city filth. Globally, slum populations are growing by 25 million people a year as poverty and lack of jobs affect more and more people. As early as the late

1990s, 1 billion workers across the globe were unemployed or underemployed. The globe grows poorer and more militarized while newly-new riches abound for the very few.

The teenage fighters of the Mahdi Army in Baghdad's Sadr City come from one of the world's largest slums.[12] The newest form of global capitalism is creating too many dispossessed and desperate people. This horrid and inhumane divide between rich and poor is the true "clash of civilizations" created by the newest versions of global capitalism.

The US's trillion-dollar wars in Afghanistan and Iraq have raged on as part of this global economy while people in those war-torn countries starve. Most recently, in January 2009 during Israel's twenty-three-day constant bombing of Gaza, more than one thousand Palestinians died, and thousands more were maimed. So many others starve. The soup kitchens in New York City cannot provide for the 1.3 million New Yorkers who are said to be hungry. Every year the city gets more racially diverse and also poorer and hungrier. How sad that so many New Yorkers should become more like slum dwellers in Mumbai while the richest people across the globe set outrageous real estate prices in Mumbai.

The destitute and the working poor increase daily in number at home and abroad and yet they are ignored or put in distant view by politicians across the globe. During the 2008 US presidential election there was no talk of America's poor. Instead the focus was on the middle class whoever that might be, except for the short period of time that Hillary spoke about the US's hard-working working class—to be distinguished from the not hard-working working class. As such, her working class was coded as white, and the poor of all colors, who are the US's working class, were silenced and forgotten once again. As unemployment continues to grow in the US we shall see how Obama chooses to name and recognize them. But I will return to all this later.

Although the American Dream has never fully worked for enough people, it has worked for many, as the Obamas repeatedly tell us. The newest global dream of a connected village is spreading to new locations in new geographical sites while it renegotiates who the haves, and have-less, and have-nots, will be. We, the ordinary everyday folk who inhabit this earth, need a new dream.

Notes

1   Louis Uchitelle, "The End of the Line As They Know It", *New York Times*, April 1, 2007, sec. 3, p. 1.
2   Pete Engardio, ed., *Chindia, How China and India Are Revolutionizing Global Business* (New York: McGraw Hill, 2007), pp. viii, ix, 50. Engardio is a senior writer with *BusinessWeek*.
3   Ibid., pp. 288, 297, 316, 323, 325.
4   William Tabb, "Four Crises of the Contemporary World Capitalist System", *Monthly Review*, vol. 60, no. 5 (October, 2008), pp. 43– 59.
5   Jodi Kantor, "Nation's Many Faces in Extended First Family", *New York Times*, January 21, 2009, p. A1.
6   Naomi Klein, *The Shock Doctrine* (New York: Metropolitan Books, 2007).
7   David Cay Johnston, *Perfectly Legal* (New York: Penguin, Portfolio, 2003), pp. 13, 16, 24, 30.
8   John Bellamy Foster, "Peak Oil and Energy Imperialism", *Monthly Review*, vol. 60, no. 3 (July/August, 2008), p. 12.
9   Fred Magdoff, "The World Food Crisis", *Monthly Review*, vol. 60, no. 1 (May, 2008), pp. 1, 3, 4.
10 For a compelling description of the punishing poverty that remains in India see Aravind Adiga, *The White Tiger* (New Delhi: Harper Collins, 2008).
11 Mike Davis, *Planet of Slums* (London: Verso, 2006), pp. 5, 10, 11, 13, 16–19.
12 Ibid., pp. 198, 201, 202, 203.

4

Gender Bending with the Globe

Gender and race—if one can even speak of these constructs in and of themselves in any separate and singular way—are always in the *process* of being defined. They are not givens but potentials in that their meanings shift, and bend, and sometimes maybe even break apart within and alongside their more seemingly unchanging "nature". Although gender and race are treated as static, which more often than not assumes that they are biological categories, their meanings meander continuously, reflecting the needs of economies, state formations and their militarist agendas, and other historical moments.

By now there are many scholars and political activists who take note of this fluidity and changeability, and yet the categories also remain in place, with static and unchangeable resonance. This "two-ness", as W. E. B. Dubois might say—fluidity and unchangeability—is at the heart of my wonderings. It is just possible that we live at a critical juncture today—where these changing constructions of racialized gender and engendered race hold out new possibility for the ultimate destabilization of race and gender as they have been traditionally established.

I might offer Hillary Clinton and/or Barack Obama as possible examples to query here. Hillary is female and white, while her race most often is not mentioned and her gender morphed into a commander-in-chief in the 2008 primaries. Depending upon who is speaking, Barack is seen as either Kenyan, or Indonesian, or mixed-race, or black, or mestizo, and so on. It has been noted that by 2042 whites will be a minority in the US, but white has many meanings. Many Latinos identify as white, as do Asians. Late nineteenth-century immigrants—Jews,

Slavs, Greeks, and Italians—were often seen as non-white, and "foreign", in similar ways to "other-than-white" immigrants today.

The edges of racial identity have become more blurred.[1] With interracial marriage, and mixings of races that are already blends of themselves through extraordinary histories of exchange and imperial acts, race has multiple meanings. My point is not that there is no race, or that Barack is not black, or that white privilege is not incredibly powerful for those who have it, and punishing to those who do not. Rather, I wish to explore the newest shifts and meanings of race and gender in order to see if there are radically new constructions and possibilities for them.

I am wondering if white privilege and gender are significantly and uniquely different than what they were in earlier form. In other words, that maybe this is a key historical moment that might actually alter the practices of gender and race so that former constructions of each are undermined and challenged in fundamentally unknown ways. As such, this may be a revolutionary or radical moment in which former gender and racial hierarchies are potentially destabilized. "Revolutionary" does not necessarily mean progressive, or radically democratic. But the possibility remains. An astrophysicist might call this a moment of "singularity"—"a state in which things become so radically different that the old rules break down and we know virtually nothing".[2]

If this is a unique moment in which to realign and reconfigure the domains of racialized gender and engendered race it can only be done with recognition of their structural, and not merely individualist, meaning. Obama's victory may have reflected and deepened just such a change in earlier formations of white privilege. The candidacies of Hillary Clinton and Sarah Palin may have reflected and instigated such gender clarity and fluidity as well: that gendered meanings and the female body are not simply one and the same.

Barack and Hillary have both relocated and redefined the sites that a black man and a white woman can occupy. This may appear to be fundamental and structural change, and it may actually be so, but it is not self-evident that it is. And race and gender are not simply parallel in this instance. Barack's candidacy evoked the demand for civil rights in a way that Hillary's did not. I do not think that gender is less controlling or limiting than race. But race and gender became pitted against one another in problematic fashion. This may have as much to do with the relationship between race and class as it does with race and gender. I will return to this discussion later.

Gender is being radically pluralized today even if it is not perfectly clear for whom this applies and matters. Of course, the promissory of success does not trickle down easily to girls laboring in offshore factories, or as enslaved sex workers, or living as refugees in war-torn areas. Nevertheless, the new promise for many more privileged women is that they can be whoever they wish to be. Yet the constraints on their choices are not put in view and they then become individually responsible for their own destiny. Women are now allowed to enter realms that were once closed to them through gender apartheid. Their entrance is assumed to mean their equality where often entry is done along firmly established hierarchical divides.

Although women have become more present in the militaries across the globe, for most of them this should not be confused with egalitarian developments. A majority of women continue to suffer sexual harassment, sexual humiliation, and rape in untold numbers in the military and in militarized zones. Entry into the military hardly means equity in these instances. Wars rage and girls and women pay a merciless price even with female officers and females holding high office. And many more women and girls toil in the sneaker factories across the globe than can afford to pay for and wear the shoes they make. Professional women in China and India forge a new global middle class while rural women in these countries become their servants.

The more gender bends, the more it also loses its clarity. It just may be that my notion of a sexual decoy—that the female body should not be simply read as one and the same as the culturally gendered body—is too clear-cut and constricting because gender can have too many meanings.[3] The more women are in the military and act as political operatives the more this reality becomes part of the changed expression of gender itself. The clarity of decoy status—that a female body should not automatically be presumed to be one and the same as a gendered woman—assumes that a female is tied to a static, unchanging and traditional conception of what a woman's gender is in the first place. The sexual decoy may simply be a newest form of gender expression.

Nations do not remain as they once were either. Countries are carved anew and the global economy disregards national borders whenever it is beneficial to do so. I think that global capital disregards gender and racial borders in similar ways. Women and girls provide the labor for the new global markets while renegotiating former familial and national borders. Global capital's greed has led to an economic crisis of unknown proportion along with an undermining of earlier patriarchal familial forms.

The greed stops at nothing, even at the cost of its own exposure. Global capital now undermines systems of patriarchal gender and racialized misogyny by its endless search for the cheapest labor. This endless search for profits—be it through oil or girls' and women's labor—reveals the many colors of the globe, which destabilizes earlier notions of white privilege for its more modern, "newest" form.

Global capitalism's gender bending may be beginning to undermine the structural requisites of earlier forms of patriarchy itself. The excesses of global capital have undermined patriarchal gender as it has been established through clear-cut public/private divides. And global capital has as a result created new viable and complex varieties of gender/s. These changes and tensions impugn earlier mutual dependencies between capitalism and misogyny. As such, gender exists in traditional patriarchal ways and it is also transforming misogyny in its more homogenous, standardized form.

Twenty-first-century global capitalism then creates the new with the old. These new-old formations of racialized gender are both changing and static; hence, they are newly-new, as in "newest", nonetheless. Women remain tied to the unrelenting sexual divisions of labor while also living lives that are less constricted by them. The constrictions are always economically thick and burdened while the globe unsettles gender and race clarity both culturally and historically.

Women are able to distance themselves from the more traditional aspects of patriarchy as they become wage earners, and sometimes earn higher salaries. Women who live within more traditional forms of patriarchy, given their poverty, find it harder to escape the burdens of patriarchal labor. Wealthy women have been able to alleviate the more punishing aspects of misogyny, and continue to do so with even greater effect. This is often done through their dumping the more punishing responsibilities for domestic labor on poorer women.

The labor of the globe is disproportionately done by people of color, especially women and girls. But the colors of women vary enormously, depending on place and geographical location. There are many more women of color in the middle classes today in China, Chile, Spain, etcetera than in earlier history. This complex nexus of economic class cuts through and within colors, races, and cultures, forming a newer racialized gendering of the global economy.

The global working class was never predominantly white, but rather colored men. Today the new working class is disproportionately girls and women doing domestic care work. It is the migrant and displaced labor of women and girls of color doing the "international transfer of care": domestic work, nursing, nannies, etcetera.[4] The care-related occupations develop with the growth of new middle classes. And yet these new workers are part of the continual migrant populations of displaced peoples, exiles, undocumented workers, traffickers, and so on. There are in the world 175 million people living outside their country of birth, and approximately 49 percent of them are women and girls. And of the 25 million persons internally displaced, 70 percent are women.[5]

There is an internal class hierarchy for women—as a gendered construct. In Shenzhen, China, there is a full imprint of global capitalism. There is an urban professional class of young women who now work for transnational companies. These women are known as "white-collar beauties" and they hire poor rural women to do their former domestic jobs. At the same time, these urban professional women are being re-feminized away from the so-called de-femininized heritage of Mao.[6]

Much attention has been paid to the way that global capital disregards national boundaries and reconstructs new global economic formations. I wish to point toward how global capital now also ignores and undermines the pre-existing borders of race and gender in new form. Gender and race and the way they connect and define each other are destabilized by the hunt for girls' and women's labor. This search pulls women into the paid labor force and public workspace while realigning their private and public spheres. The clear-cut divide between home and work is undermined by new global formations.

As women traverse both realms, sometimes freely, other times under coercion, the borderlines of established patriarchal gender morph. As such, gender fluidity and its bending underpin the newest globe. Global capital re-genders and maybe un-genders labor while re-sexing it. This does not mean that greater equality exists for women and girls, but it means that there is more sexual fluidity.

New forms of genders and their practices allow more flexibility although it is not at all clear whether this flexibility challenges the privileging of sexual hierarchy and sexual differentiation. Although many women have more choices today than their mothers did, there are also greater economic inequalities and therefore greater burdens to bear. Because class divisions differentiate genders and races these latter *appear* to have more diversity, and possibly fluidity. Hillary can be Secretary of State but it is not at all clear what this means for the rest of women, both in the US and elsewhere.

The new excesses of wealth appear to create new expressions and possibly fluidities of gender. So gender, and with it race, become more complex and differentiated and diverse. This new complexity may say little about the fundamental structural shifts of patriarchal gender and racial privilege for the masses. Or it may possibly undermine the historical limitations used to discipline and regulate women's lives.

Please do not misunderstand my querying here. I do not think patriarchy or white privilege or misogyny will wither away in consequence of the assaults of global capitalism. Rather, I think that global capitalism destabilizes genders and races as we have known them, and will do its best to reformulate them for its new/est needs. I rather point to several other important claims: that the new fluidity and diversity within the constructs of gender and race should not be misinterpreted as though they mean civil and women's rights have been achieved; that existing constructs of racism and sexism need new political conceptualization; that these new complexities prove that race and gender are endlessly malleable and therefore open to all kinds of new regressive and progressive possibility; that gender and race are both newly punishing, and not.

In sum: countries are more racially diverse and mixed than they used to be during colonialism, when the mother country often remained white. Today, a country like the US is richly colored and racially diverse, with people from all over the globe. As well, gender today is more differentiated and complex. More economic differences exist within engendered misogyny. Although women have always inhabited countries, in a way that multiple races have not, the spaces women occupy have become more differentiated in labor markets.

Yet women's presence, even their new majority status in the US labor force, should not be confused with gender equality. Because of the US economic downturn, women for the first time in history surpass men in the labor force. Eighty-two percent of the job losses have affected men, not women. Gendered job losses, and not gender equity, explains women's newest economic standing. And this standing bespeaks the inequity and poor pay of the jobs that women in the US remain mired in, now as heads of households.[7]

All this said, the incredible pluralism of choice that challenges the glass ceilings remains possible for a precious few. And in this sense, radically plural genders and races continue to be embedded in white privilege and misogynist hierarchy for the masses of poor people across the globe. Yet, alongside these limitations, I also continue to look to find and see the newest racialized gender and gendered racial formations for their possibilities to enliven a politics of a newly radical democracy.

Notes

1   Sam Roberts, "A Nation of None and All of the Above", *New York Times*, August 17, 2008, p. wk6.
2   P. W. Singer, *Wired for War* (New York: Penguin Press, 2009), p. 102.
3   See my *Sexual Decoys, Gender, Race and War in Imperial Democracy* (London: Zed Books, 2007), especially chapters 1 and 2, for a full discussion of my use of the term 'sexual decoy'.
4   Robyn Magalit Rodriquez, "The Labor Brokerage State and the Globalization of Filipina Care Workers", *Signs*, vol. 33, no. 4 (Summer, 2008), p. 795.
5   Adele Jones, "A Silent but Mighty River: The Costs of Women's Economic Migration", *Signs*, vol. 33, no. 4 (Summer, 2008), pp. 761, 762.
6   Zhongxin Sun, "Worker, Woman, Mother: Redefining Urban Chinese Women's Identity via Motherhood and the Global Workplace", *Asian Journal of Women's Studies*, vol. 14, no. 1 (2008), pp. 7–33.
7   Catherine Rampell, "US Women Set to Surpass Men in Labor Force", *New York Times*, February 6, 2009, p. A7.

5

Global Capitalist Crises

It has been known for about a decade now—roughly the duration of the Bush/Cheney regime—that the richest have been getting still richer and everybody else has been working harder for less. Income inequality in the US has increased. Wages have stagnated. The number of people uninsured for health care has risen significantly. Unemployment has passed 7 percent. The price of gas remains doubled. The cost of food is soaring. Financial markets are near collapse.

More than half a million people in the US lost their jobs in November 2008, alone. By January 2009 more than 11 million were unemployed, with millions more underemployed. More than 2.6 million jobs were lost during 2007. All told, about 21 million people—that means one in every eight workers—across gender and racial divides were jobless or underemployed as Obama began his office.

The US public is told that our very own rich tycoons have broken every law, avoided every regulation, and created global chaos. The economic turmoil hits markets everywhere across the globe, and US banks and financiers are responsible for much of the blame.[1] If anyone were speaking the truth it would be said that capitalism is an unconscionable, corrupted, and inhumane system. And there would be truth and reconciliation hearings at which the thieves could confess their crimes.

Exxon Mobil made nearly $1,500 per second in the second quarter of 2008: that is, a net income of $11.68 billion on revenues of $138 billion. The richest get richer and Americans on the whole remain resigned to this injustice. People are driving less, buying motor scooters and using bicycles more than before, while knowing and also denying that the US is on a downward slide. Millions, then billions, and now trillions have been spent funding the unfixable Iraq War, and life at home seems, and is, ever more unmanageable for greater numbers of people across the racial and class spectrum. There are 'newly-new' gender and racial mappings to be found and reckoned with across the globe.

The present US economic crisis was unveiled to the public by some of its very own architects. The ineffectual president Bush addressed the US public declaring the immediate need for American taxpayers to stand behind our failed financial institutions in order to avert a total economic collapse. Initially, the US House of Representatives failed to approve a bailout for Wall Street that was proposed by Henry Paulson, the Treasury Secretary and Ben Bernanke, the Federal Reserve chairman.

Over two hundred economists wrote an open letter to Congress asking that the bailout not be approved without grave revision. Eventually a slightly revised "compromise" package that promised some few restraints on the greedy was passed by the Senate. Naomi Klein called this "a final frantic looting of the public wealth before they hand over the keys to the safe". The package has "tethered" the public interest to private companies while "turning the state into a giant insurance agency for Wall Street".[2]

The US is facing an economic crisis of the "newest" proportions as I write. Since the market peak on October 9, 2007 the stock market has fallen 19.6 percent. Several firms in crisis were bailed out: Bear Stearns, for $29 billion, American International Group, for $85 billion, and Fannie Mae/Freddie Mac for $200 billion. Lehman Brothers was left to sink on its own.[3] It should not be left unsaid that Republican presidential hopeful John McCain's campaign manager was receiving regular $15,000 payments from the failed mortgage company Freddie Mac. Nor that Henry Paulson is the former CEO of Goldman Sachs which had favored status with the bailout, leading to what William Greider calls "Goldman Sachs Socialism".[4] Nor should it be left silenced that huge payoffs, even if not bailouts *per se*, are integral to the usual spending of our government on any given day. This outrageous spending is especially true of everyday defense and military expenditures.

According to Chalmers Johnson a 2008 defense bill includes $68.6 billion to continue the wars in Afghanistan and Iraq. He argues that the money is pure waste—for our "extravagantly expensive failed wars abroad". On September 24, 2008, while the fight over the billions of taxpayer dollars that were to bail out Wall Street was in process, the House of Representatives passed a $612 billion defense authorization bill for 2009 with no public scrutiny, or vetting by the press.[5] This defense spending reveals a government hemorrhaging by its own hand, a spectacle that is still extraordinary no matter how often it happens.

The corporate bailouts that mimic the wastefulness of military spending are crucial to the continued functioning of the newest forms of global capitalism. The military budget of $700 billion in 2007 rivals the initial estimates of the bailout package.[6] Meanwhile, the US wastes $12 billion a month on its wars in Iraq and Afghanistan. The travesty in Iraq may end up costing some $3 trillion, while the US accounts for 45 percent of the world's military expenditures. Meanwhile its poor children, along with Iraq's children, go hungry.

The US taxpayer, who is the flip side of government spending, is asked to bail out Wall Street bankers and financiers to the tune of over $800 million—although several economists estimate that the real bill at the end of this road could range between 2 and 7 trillion dollars. This government spending is a giveaway to Wall Street with little to no governmental enforcement, or oversight, or regulation. Meanwhile world leaders, one after the other, spoke at the United Nations of their fears for the entire global market as it was expected that a "staggering 50 million" people would be jobless by the end of 2009.[7]

President Luiz Inácio Lula da Silva of Brazil stated in his opening remarks to the UN, "We must not allow the burden of the boundless greed of a few to be shouldered by all."[8] It helps nothing that the spiraling collapse of the US financial system is spoken of as though it has a life of its own—the natural, even divine, self-propulsion of markets is used by neo-liberals like Paulson and Alan Greenspan (Treasury Secretary and Federal Reserve Chairman respectively under George W. Bush) to absolve themselves of responsibility. The American taxpayer is told that no one really comprehends what has happened: not the Security and Exchange Commission, not the Federal Deposit Insurance Corporation, not the Secretary of the Treasury, and not the Federal Reserve. Now in hindsight, it is revealed that no one was overseeing and assessing the "newest" systems of credit, and loans, and mortgages.

These financial gimmicks were crafted as a new risky "casino capitalism".[9] The real values of assets were unknown and also falsified. These "newest" forms of lending and unregulated risktaking were unknowns with unknown outcomes. Value had never been brokered on such terms before. Bernard Madoff, the rogue US financier that swindled thousands of his investors of billions of dollars and left many people financially ruined, represents the worst of this fallacious moneymaking. But Madoff aside, there is much blame to go around. Significant parts of the economy—from realtors to bankers to stockholders to everyday investors—were complicit in the Wall Street scamming. Obama's economic stimulus package is caught up in this financially contradictory maze.

The crisis is critical because those who created it have no conscience. They did not care about the effects of the leveraging and crediting and masquerading that they used on ordinary people. There is something especially obscene about manipulating a person's need for a home, creating and necessitating a housing bubble that makes the homes too difficult to afford, and then forcing these same people to default, and then to be foreclosed. Ordinary people came to know "new" and unknown wealth, debt, insecurity, and vulnerability.

The full story here is deeply ugly. The so-called mortgage crisis for some is as much about deindustrialization and job loss as it is about houses. New mortgages were often extended to people who had already paid off their home loans but who had lost their jobs. In Akron, Ohio, serious job loss occurred especially in poor black neighborhoods after the three rubber giants—Goodyear, Goodrich, and Firestone—closed their plants. People who could not find jobs were continuously being asked whether they wanted a new mortgage. Remortgaging homes became a substitute for needed wages. And the mortgage payments got way too big. Addie Polk, who had remortgaged and then was unable to keep up with her payments, instead of becoming homeless, shot herself on her eviction day.[10]

Debt, rather than capital, defines the leftovers of this corrupt set of economic policies. A vicious cycle arises called "the paradox of deleveraging". Economist Paul Krugman argues that if the US government is going to provide capital to these failed firms it should get a share in the ownership so that the "gains if the rescue plan works don't go to the people who made the mess in the first place". This is in clear opposition to Paulson's insistence that he needed a "clean plan" with "no strings attached".[11]

The economic crisis and its possible remedy eventually engulfed the 2008 presidential election. McCain at first said that the economy was sound, a statement he came to regret. Then he spoke with the *Wall Street Journal* saying that he is "always for less regulation". Next he mimicked his longtime economic advisor Phil Gramm, saying that the economic crisis was "psychological". Finally he called for "regulatory oversight and transparency and accountability of Wall Street".[12]

During the presidential campaign Obama consistently called for better regulation and oversight, more protection for home-owners, and a promise of greater accountability by Wall Street. He repeatedly critiqued the old "trickle-down ideology" of laissez-faire markets and governments. And he spoke of the need for a stimulus package that creates jobs and assists homeowners. He even applauded "spreading the wealth around" because it can be good for everybody.

It did not take the Republican vice-presidential candidate Sarah Palin very long to label Obama a socialist for his sentiments about spreading the wealth. (If only he were.) However, it is interesting to note that much of Palin's popularity as governor of Alaska comes from the fact that she is a "spreader" herself: a kind of "socialist with an Alaskan face". The state she governs has no income or sales tax because it "imposes huge levies on the oil companies that lease its oil fields. The proceeds finance the government's activities" and allow a yearly check to each man, woman, and child in the state. In 2007 every Alaskan received a bigger check than usual—$3,269, given the high price of oil at the time. Alaskans collectively own the resources, and they share in the wealth.[13]

The American public did not seem to worry too much about whether Obama was a socialist or not, and sided with him, most likely because his challenge to Wall Street and the greed of neo-liberal capitalists was measured, and hardly socialist. The real issue of capitalism's excessive inequalities was not brought center stage and the financial crisis was treated as an aberration of a greedy few, instead of as the normal functioning of capitalism with its unbridled maximization of profit.

Yet a more sustainable economic plan must be found if the globe is not to implode. Climate crisis, income disparity, horrific poverty, human disease, water scarcity, clean water, and energy insecurity are integral parts of this global economic crisis. They do not exist separately from capitalism's excesses, and Wall Street ignores these relationships at all of our peril. If we address the interconnectedness of these crises maybe the planet can become a more habitable place for ordinary people.

Michael Moore says in wonderfully clear fashion that no one anymore wants the out-dated cars that General Motors, Chrysler and Ford make. They are wasteful, harmful to the planet, and too expensive to run. He suggests that instead of bailing out the auto companies, they should be bought outright and then run by people who will really commit to the needed technologies that respect the planet. Moore suggests that a government-run company could make the trains, and subways, and buses we all need. There would be better transport and plenty of new jobs instead of more layoffs to insure the Big Three's profits. As Moore says: "These idiots don't deserve a dime. Fire all of them and take over the industry for the good of the workers, the country and the planet."[14] It is, after all, ordinary working- and middle-class people that deserve to be bailed out here. Moore was giddily thrilled when Obama eventually fired Rick Wagoner, the CEO of General Motors.

Sustainable agriculture and biodiversity must also be at the top of the list of concerns. Since 2006 the average world price for rice has increased by 217 percent, wheat by 136 percent, corn by 125 percent and soybeans by 107 percent. These food prices mean human starvation for a massive number of people across the globe. This is why food insecurity must be recognized as an urgent problem, and food sovereignty must be recognized and respected as a human right. The "protection of rural environments—fish stocks, landscapes, food traditions based on ecologically sustainable management of lands, soils, water, seas, seeds, livestock and other biodiversity", needs immediate recognition.[15] To the extent that these concerns are ignored in the discussions of the present economic crisis, too many of the globe's needs are silenced with them.

One of the saddest and most harmful effects of the present financial collapse for the US is that it may make it harder for Obama to get the support he needs to challenge the crisis mentality that underpins neoliberalism. Although one might hope that the ongoing tragedy of Wall Street would embolden a new embrace of governmental democratically poised action and a commitment to the public's good, it may instead bolster the scarcity mentality that leads to further neoliberalism, privatization and natural resource mismanagement and depletion. With so much newly new and extraordinary debt already in place, expectations for universal health care, subsidized college loans, infrastructure investment, price controls on food and gas, increased unemployment benefits, may be more easily sidelined.

Obama has his plate full in terms of needs needing to be met, and empty in terms of available funds to make this all happen. The US is already in dire shape given the past decades of neoliberal privatization leading to new forms of fascistic democracy under Bush and Cheney. A recent report by the American Society of Civil Engineers states that the US's infrastructure is failing and needs at least $1.6 trillion to bring it up to par. According to the report nearly 30 percent of the nation's 590,750 bridges are "structurally deficient or functionally obsolete". More than 33 percent of dams were found to be unsafe. The US's water supply needs immediate attention and public transportation also needs a complete overhaul.[16]

It should be no surprise that there is no quick fix to be found, or why Congress initially failed to pass the bailout package, 228 to 205. Forty percent of Democrats and two thirds of Republicans said no. And what a strange mix of politics: the Democrats speaking as populists to protect the people on Main Street and the Republicans speaking as free market capitalists. A compromise was in the making because this is what politicians do. But the US government will not remain the same, and nor will the economy, although what the changes will be are yet to unfold.

There is something newly new about this economic crisis. There is a terror in the air for millions of poor and starving people, both in the US and across the globe. The world feels more dangerous because of capitalism's excesses, rather than because of Islamic "terrorists". And it is the poor and working poor who need recognition and redress, not simply the middle class.

I cannot help but keep wondering if this newly new economic geography is part and parcel of the newly gendered and newly racial makeup of the global economy. Women of all colors of the working class have been hurt the hardest by the sub-prime mortgage disaster in the US. Women of color remain the poorest of the poor across the globe while at the same time women of many colors occupy new locations of power, as presidents and even four-star generals. Women are pulled and pushed into new practices—from cabinet members to sexual trafficking to factory girls, to CEOs. These variegated forms bespeak astounding change *and* also stagnant statisticity.

Because the economic inequality of the globe is so ignored, and because women and girls still remain disproportionately the poor everywhere, the gendered aspects of the global economic crisis are most often unrecognized and unnamed. So also as usual the racial structuring of both gender and economic class is unrecognized, and put aside. It should be noted that most of the financial overseers of the global economic crisis are men, and they are disproportionately white. But given all I have written about the porousness and changeability of race and gender I will not make too much of this point.

Despite their newly new fluidity, the gender and racial mappings across the globe that I mention also remain historically stagnant and limiting for the majority of people across the globe. While a very few white women and even fewer women and men of color "newly" rule, the majority toil. And this majority— across race and gender—continues to be defined by problematic economic class divides. So I am more than curious about what Michelle and Barack will and can do.

Notes

1   For an interesting discussion of the role of banks in creating the economic disaster of the 1930s Great Depression see: Liaquat Ahamed, *Lords of Finance* (New York: Penguin Press, 2009).

2   Naomi Klein, "The Bailout: Bush's Final Pillage", *The Nation*, vol. 287, no. 16 (November 17, 2008), p. 10.

3   Edmund Andrews, "Bush Officials Urge Swift Action on Broad Rescue Powers", *New York Times*, September 20, 2008, p. A1.

4   William Greider, "Goldman Sachs Socialism", *The Nation*, vol. 287, no. 11 (October 13, 2008), p. 5.

5   Chalmers Johnson, "We Have the Money", Asia Times online, September 30, 2008, www.atimes.com. Also see his *Nemesis: The Last Days of the American Republic* (New York: Metropolitan Books, 2006).

6   John Bellamy Foster, Hannah Holleman, and Robert McChesney, "The U.S. Imperial Triangle and Military Spending", *Monthly Review*, vol. 60, no. 5 (October, 2008), p. 1.

7   Nelson D. Schwartz, "Unemployment Surges around the World, Threatening Stability", *New York Times*, February 16, 2009, p. A1.

8   President Lula quoted in Neil MacFarquhar, "Upheaval on Wall St. Stirs Anger in the UN", *New York Times*, September 20, 2008, p. A6.

9   Robert Pollin, "Ending Casino Capitalism", *The Nation*, vol. 287, no. 11 (October 13, 2008), p.7

10   Peter Boyer, "Eviction", *The New Yorker*, November 24, 2008, pp.48-53.

11   Paul Krugman, "Cash for Trash", *New York Times*, September 22, 2008, p. A23.

12   Editorial, *The Nation*, vol. 287, no. 10 (September 17, 2008), p. 3.

13   Hendrik Hertzberg, "Like, Socialism", *The New Yorker*, November 3, 2008, pp. 43, 46.

14   Michael Moore, "A Message from Michael Moore", December 3, 2008.

15   Brian Ashley, "Free the Food not the Markets", *Amandla!*, Issue no. 2 (June/July, 2008), p. 10.

16   Felix Rohatyn and Everett Ehrlich, "A New Bank to Save Our Infrastructure", *The New York Review of Books*, Vol. LX, no. 15 (October 9, 2008), p. 27.

6

Chinua Achebe and Listening to Africa

Obama's father was from Kenya, Africa. Barack Obama Senior was born on the shores of Lake Victoria near Kendu Bay. He was a member of the Luo tribe. He herded goats as a boy and after attended school in Nairobi and then in Hawaii. He worked as an economist for much of his life when he returned to Kenya. Not much of his story has been told. He died in a car crash in Nairobi in 1982 when he was forty-six years old.[1]

Obama only knew his father for a brief time, and then he was gone. Kenyans danced in the streets with joy when Obama won the US presidency. But in a world which for the most part ignores Africans and their stories, the fact that Obama's father was absent for most of his life only serves to make Africa even more remote, however noisy the clamor around the Obama biography.

Chinua Achebe was baptized Albert Chinuaalumogu. Echoing W. E. B. Dubois before him, Achebe says that we cannot afford not to listen to and hear and see Africa's nearly 1 billion people. Achebe grew up in Ogidi, Nigeria, within a colonial classroom, struggling against the colonial gaze. He tells his readers that they cannot know much if they are not straining to know Africa, and with it the humanity of the globe. He writes against the dehumanization of Africa and its trauma of dispossession. Africa was "never completely human" under colonial eyes and Achebe has dedicated his life and writing to exposing and interrogating this truth.[2]

He insists that people inhabiting colonial empires must work harder at listening and understanding the colonized. They must insist on hearing the whisperings and finding the shadows that lurk behind the obvious. Achebe writes in English although he is bilingual but says, "Let no one be fooled by the fact that we may write in English for we intend to do unheard of things with it". He reminds us that we must read and listen, and think very carefully. And that careful thinking always requires resistance and a critical curiosity. He believes that literature has the obligation to undo and "exorcise the ghosts of colonialism" because it has been so complicit in dehumanizing the African continent.[3] Achebe writes as an act of defiant living, as a claim on his own humanity against its continual colonial dehumanization.

The colonial mind, if allowed, depends on and necessitates the inhuman status of the peoples of Africa. They are seen as a kind of primordial barbarity, while Europe is viewed as a form of progress and goodness. Achebe says that Europeans fear the common ancestry and humanity of humankind and therefore destroy it through their own barbarism. Likened to Thomas Hobbes, Achebe describes the world as frightful and endlessly at war. Achebe chuckles while changing Hobbes's often-quoted colonial words a bit. For Achebe the world becomes "nasty, British, and short", rather than the original "nasty, brutish, and short". In fear Westerners run from self-encounters and develop the fiction of racial superiority to justify them. The horror is that racial superiority is a "malignant fiction" that is taken to be true. And truth here is little else than a painful and punishing fantasy.[4]

Achebe displaces the everyday solipsism of uncareful living. He demands that we doubt universals because they most often are overdrawn generalizations about exclusionary specifics. Universals simply thematize the world from the viewpoint of a power-filled gaze, excluding ordinary people. And the universals almost always exist as exclusive of Africans. Colonialist discourse with whiteness as its gaze, means that racism is a punishing impediment. For Achebe, Western privilege must find a new humility of discovery for listening.

The spatial meanings of colonial empire are continuously shifting and changing alongside the contours of gender and race. Amy Kaplan names this process "manifest domesticity", which turns an imperial nation into a home; which calls "distance from home" foreign; which defines ever shifting new out-posts and locations as "others".[5] It is more than significant that Mark Twain found parallels between the colonization of Hawaii and the "violence of slavery" and the slave-holding South. According to Kaplan, Twain's visit to Hawaii revealed "a nightmare of slavery" and the anxieties about the capacities of "non-whites", as well as the irony of "freeing-free men".[6] I think about the shadows of "othering" for Obama, who was born in Kansas and grew up mixed-race in Hawaii.

Obama continues to mobilize people with his belief in and talk about "hope". Achebe writes as much about hope as Obama, but also writes of hope's impediments. Achebe chides the white man for "talking and talking and never listening because he imagines he has been talking to a dumb beast. You may talk to a horse but you don't wait for a reply." Whites simulate dialogue when they really carry on a monologue with themselves. Achebe concludes that in confronting the black, the white has a "simple choice: either to accept the black man's humanity and the equality that flows from it; or to reject it and see him as a beast of burden". For Achebe, there is no middle ground.[7] For Obama there usually is.

Long before the present "wars of/on terror", Achebe warned that if a president pursues a terrorist, the two become indistinguishable.[8] Long before Obama became president, Achebe was warning that colonial minds do not know how to think very well, or how to listen carefully. Let us hope that Obama will share in Achebe's directives when he reminds us that the humanity of Africa must be truly listened to. This means standing against the wars that betray people's faith in themselves and others; that turn young girls into empty shells of what they once were. As Achebe writes, "the sickness of war eats at our souls"; having sex in wartime is similar to "shelling" and life in general has gotten "maggoty at the center".[9]

Chinua Achebe makes clear that for too long the US has

carried on a monologue with itself. Dialogue is instead needed—especially with the countries and cultures found in Africa. Before real listening can happen, equality must be granted. Without equality, these voices in and of Africa cannot be fully heard. Equality is essential in order to hear and see another. And this remains an important truth both within and outside the US. People from all over the world already reside inside the US, which makes borders more porous than before, although still punishing. This tension between colonialism and its changing forms further demands recognizing that hopefulness is always lessened by a realistic recognition of impediments.[10]

The contours of identity are multilayered and permeable. Recognizing this pluralism of identity and its complexities challenges neat and knowable contours and borders. And when the inside/outside divide is understood as both fluid and also starkly punishing the notion of hopefulness is tempered and also extended to new possibilities. Obama says that it is only in America that his story—starting with a black Kenyan father and white Christian mother from Kansas—could unfold. This statement, though repeated often, is probably not helpfully valid. He sees impediments everywhere else, and lessens the limitations in the US too much. His story could happen elsewhere and his story of opportunity and success does not happen here often enough.

The US House of Representatives formally apologized for the injustices of slavery and Jim Crow laws on July 29, 2008.[11] The apology is focused on past history. Memory is always important. Twelve US presidents owned slaves, and eight of them did so while holding office.[12] Yes, much has changed since then.

I still wonder about the present, with its racial and gendered inequities and injustices. Though the present is much improved, racial indignities and punishments remain and continue. Obama's election is enormously hopeful and hope-filled and yet it does not bespeak an end of racism. It does, however, augur a new racial moment.

This kind of change, bespeaking the old alongside the new, is reminiscent of the end of South African racial apartheid, in that so much has been altered and yet too much remains the same. The US must stay focused on Africa to ensure that this extraordinary moment is not used to cover over voices that we must hear. Achebe is unrelenting in reminding anyone who is willing to listen that an embrace of human dignity in Africa must always prevail in our life's undertakings.

There are new dialogues with colonialism and racism to be found that take us beyond the triumphs of Nelson Mandela and Obama. Structural racism, in the form of racial apartheid and/or global imperialism, morph and re-form. The re-formations are both hugely liberating and also horribly punishing. The most democratic constitution in the world is enshrined on the continent of Africa—in South Africa. The people of the globe should never forget this. But constitutions are not enough.

Breyten Breytenbach writes critically of Mandela's compromises and longingly of a free Africa. He imagines "a continent that will develop its own sustainable modernity far away from Western 'universal' models of globalization serving only the masters". He yearns for an African integrity that does not "blackmail or whitemail" itself or the world; that will "eradicate small arms and have no purpose for acquiring submarines". He begs the continent "to think against hegemony of any variety", and "the idolization" of its leaders. And he reminds us all not to be "obedient citizens" because "our absolute loyalty lies in the disobedience to power and in our identification with the poor".[13]

I agree. It is not helpful to idolize Barack Obama, or Mandela, or any political leader. The other side of idolatry is a passive obedience. The US at this moment of hopefulness instead needs what my friend the Iranian scholar Hamid Dabashi calls loyal opposition.

Notes

1   Barack Obama, *Dreams from My Father* (New York: Three Rivers Press, 1995), p. 9.
2   Chinua Achebe, *Home and Exile* (New York: Anchor Books, 2000), pp. 24, 49, 79.
3   Achebe quoted in Ruth Franklin, "After Empire", *New Yorker,* May 26, 2008, pp. 75, 76.
4   Chinua Achebe, *Hopes and Impediments: Selected Essays, 1965–87* (London: Heinemann, 1988), pp. 8, 12, 76, 79, 140–45, 146, 148.
5   Amy Kaplan, *The Anarchy of Empire in the Making of US Culture* (Cambridge, MA: Harvard University Press, 2002), pp. 13, 15, 23, 50.
6   Ibid., pp. 75, 76, 85, 91.
7   Achebe, *Home and Exile*, pp.15, 19.
8   Ibid., p.55.
9   Chinua Achebe, *Girls at War and Other Stories* (New York: Random, 1972), pp. 109, 115, 116.
10 Chinua Achebe, *Hopes and Impediments* (New York: Anchor Books, 1988).
11 House Resolution 194, http://thomas.loc.gov
12 David Remnick, "Comment: Homelands", *New Yorker*, January 12, 2009, p. 17.
13 Breyten Breytenbach, "Mandela's Smile", *Harper's Magazine*, December, 2008, p. 48.

7

The Newest China and Her Olympics

The 2008 US presidential election was written with and on the globe; and the globe and its economic tumult were threaded through the election. As the newest market-driven machinations of the globe unfold, so does US politics. Post-Olympics China is suffering an economic downturn: exports declined starting in October/November 2008.[1] Yet it (inconsistently) vied for its place as a new global player at the economic summit in London, April 2009, while making plans to become the world leader in producing electric cars.[2]

It has been said that the 2008 Olympics was China's coming-out party as modern and capitalist and the new leader of the global economy. According to Thomas Friedman, the building of this "magnificent $43 billion infrastructure" was the "culmination of seven years of national investment, planning, concentrated state power, national mobilization and hard work". China was awarded the games just shortly before September 11, 2001. So while China was building better subways, roads, airports and parks, we were "building better metal detectors and armored humvees".

But it has not been a simple walk in the park for China. She has been found to be producing unsafe lead-contaminated children's toys and infant formula laced with melamine. Four infants died from traces of melamine and another 54,000 suffered kidney ailments. It was a national tragedy.

Nevertheless, newly modernized sites in China have surpassed the sophistication of the US. The new international airport is spacious, and dazzling with sunlight; makes Westerners feel like they have been left in the dust with our decrepit infrastructure.[3]

The main Olympic stadium—nicknamed the Bird's Nest—with its fabulous architectural visions stands in homage to the success of Beijing as a fashionable global city. Times change and China is now called the "new" China.

Its economic upsurge and newest economic strength are embodied in the imagery of the 2008 Olympic Games. China led with 51 gold medals, more than any other nation has ever accumulated, "and it was time for others to emulate her, rather than the other way around".[4] For the moment, forget that it is not always easy to decipher where nations begin or end: China had scoured the globe for coaches for its Olympic teams and US gymnasts had a Chinese coach.

The newest architecture, infrastructure, and surveillance techniques imported from the US make China modern and competitive and "first world", so to speak. China's huge and successful expenditure on the games became the newest success story for global capital. Cutthroat competition now rules almost everywhere. Losers are defined by hair-splits of a second. Winner takes all. Michael Phelps became a multi-millionaire and was excessively covered by media as the golden boy until he was caught inhaling pot. All the other superathletes faded into the backdrop, much like ordinary, everyday people fade into the background in daily life.

Not everyone is as laudatory as Friedman about the Chinese government's choices and planning. Others think that the "surface sheen" of the Olympics created the usual "imagery of cosmetic face-lifts" rather than significant urban planning. Despite the forward-looking brilliance of the original architectural vision, hundreds of thousands of people were displaced by the Olympic construction with no long-term plan for the needs of the public in mind. The Olympics bespeaks the "reckless embrace of the fashionable and the global" alongside "authoritarian planning heedless of human cost".[5] It also justified huge spending for building what Naomi Klein terms a "high tech police state" to provide for the safety and security of the games and its athletes. Most of this surveillance apparatus that was designed with the assist of US defense contractors now stays in place for the long-term.

This $13 billion security extravaganza is justified as "anti-terror security" and has become a part of China's modernized authoritarianism. "The global homeland security business is worth an estimated 200 billion dollars." These global/local endeavors continue to renegotiate national borders, so China, with its Starbucks and Kentucky Fried Chicken, on the surface looks more like the US, and the US becomes more like China in our wiretapping and torture.[6] And the two economies become more enmeshed as the Chinese government invests money in the US to keep from inflation at home and to keep a lid on its economy. Without China's billion-dollars-a-day subsidy, the US could not keep its economy from total collapse.[7] These permeable economic borders mean that China also holds around $1 trillion in US Treasury notes and Fannie Mae and Freddie Mac bonds.

The broadcaster NBC set itself up in Beijing to narrate and spectacularize China's economic success story to the rest of the world. Nevertheless, we were also continually reminded of Chinese human rights violations and the lack of Chinese protest demonstrations and protestors alike. The message: China might be advancing economically, but politically it remains closed, authoritarian, and repressive. Although this critique of China is in part accurate, it is also true that the US has become more like China in this arena.

The US under Bush/Cheney became more authoritarian and repressive and without a progressive vision. It is significant although complicated that Barack Obama, while still a candidate for the US presidency, said that if he were president during the Olympics he might boycott the opening ceremonies to bring attention to the problem of human rights. Chinese youth did not take kindly to this. In contrast, president Bush attended the ceremonies and seemed more at home than usual while outside the US. He was having a good time given all the sports.

The US media negativity towards China's record on human rights creates a new kind of Chinese nationalism, especially among some youth, who are called "fen ging". They become patriotic in a defensive posture, "and instead of embracing the West, or the liberal democracy of the Tiananmen Square protesters in 1989, they speak of China's sovereignty and prosperity".[8] Yet, if asked who their hero is they say Bill Gates, not Chairman Mao. This nationalism, which is deeply rooted in an embrace of the global economy, is captured in the phrase "China can say no". Nine out of ten Chinese, when asked shortly after the Olympics whether they approve of the way things are going in China, said that they do. This support is a lot more than the 22 percent of citizens who, near the end of Bush/Cheney's term, thought the US was headed in the right direction.

Ted Koppel of PBS named China the "People's Republic of Capitalism" in his TV special documentary in July 2008. At this time China was growing its economy, not shrinking it. The Chinese government invests in infrastructure—from highways to education—which facilitates its march forward. All students are required to study biology, chemistry and physics, while only 18 percent of the students in the US do so. China is grooming a new, even if different kind of middle class, as the US did years ago during the 1950s. The numbers in China are daunting. Thirty-five thousand new citizens go online for the first time daily. Their middle class is 350 million strong and projected to become 700 million by 2020. Although much poverty remains in this more than billion person country, these numbers mark significant change.

China is the world's main manufacturer. Of the planet's 193 nations it is first in the production of coal, steel and cement. It produces half of the world's cameras and one third of the televisions. It is also the largest consumer of coal, grain, cell phones and TV sets. It uses more coal than the US, Russia, and India combined. It uses half of the world's steel and concrete and probably will construct half of the world's new buildings over the next decade. On the other end, it supplies 30 percent of the international furniture trade while deforesting the land and speeding up climate change. This despoiling of the soil is part of China's and the US's high consumption/high waste model.

Four fifths of the lengths of China's rivers are too polluted for fish to survive and half of the population, approximately 600 to 700 million people, drink water contaminated with animal and human waste. Whole forests are succumbing to China's consumption of 45 billion pairs of chopsticks per year.[9] And, given China's coal-fired power plants, much of the particulate pollution over Los Angeles originates in China.[10]

Then, however "new" the new China is, it is also very old. It follows the established rules of global capital. The rich are getting very rich, and for now there is also a growing middle class, but alongside a desperate and huge class of urban and rural poor. In the US, we have passed through and seem to have left the moment when the middle class grows. But before concluding this point, I am not sure about all this talk of the middle class in the first place. The middle class, in many ways, is simply the better-paid part of the working class. For a short while in the 2008 presidential primaries it seemed as though Hillary might have understood this.

Most US media coverage of the Olympics shuts out China's five million newly homeless people and their surrounds, devastated by the Sichuan earthquake just months before the games. More than 80,000 people perished that day. China, despite its Olympics grandeur, is also its poor and huddled masses. It is also a country that gets 31 percent of its oil from Africa, and is a main trading partner with and importer of raw materials from this continent. As a consequence of this, China is a major benefactor of the war in Sudan as it supplies the Janjawiid with oil revenue to buy guns, which are then also supplied by China. China simultaneously finances large projects in Sudan and uses its own workers to build infrastructure for oil pipelines. And, because the US keeps tight control over oil supplies elsewhere, she pushes China to deal with the Sudan as well as Iraq.[11]

Given all this global interweaving, nations become global conglomerates. It is primarily out-of-country transnational firms that make up the industry of China that now dominates China's export activity. High-tech goods are assembled in China but the parts and components are imported. China simply provides the labor. In 2003, "foreign-invested firms" produced "ninety percent of the computers, components, and peripherals" that were exported from China.[12]

These global flows and economic conditions define Wal-Mart, which has become the second-largest company in the world, second only to Exxon-Mobil. Its revenues in 2006 were worth $315 billion, with profits of more than $11 billion. It boasts 1.8 million employees while instituting wage caps for long-term employees and providing no health insurance for more than 46 percent of its workers' children worldwide. Many of its US workers have to rely on public assistance programs—given that an average salary for a sales clerk in 2006 was $13,861 a year—that cost taxpayers millions of dollars each year. Lee Scott, Wal-Mart's president and CEO, made $17.7 million in 2006—that is, 2000 times the wages of an average employee. These newest extremes have finally led to economic collapse and crisis for the globe.

The new global economic crisis deeply affects Wal-Mart which depends completely on Chinese labor and on the goods that are produced in China. Each year Wal-Mart purchases $15 billion worth of products from China. There would be no Wal-Mart without Chinese laborers. It uses over 3,000 Chinese factories to produce its goods, almost as many factories as it has stores in the US. As economic borders become more fluid with and between nations and their corporations, so do the constructions of gender and race.

The richest person in China in 2006 was a woman, Cheung Yan, the 50-something-year-old owner of Nine Dragons Paper which imports US waste paper for recycling. The US exports garbage to China and China recycles it for the globe. In the process a female rises to the top of China's economy with an initial worth of $3.4 billion. Her wealth grew alongside the poverty of millions of new Chinese girl laborers—the *dagonmei*—in the newest factories. In 2007 Cheung Yan's wealth grew to more than $10 billion and she was said to be "the richest self-made woman in the world". But her fortune has plummeted with the worldwide economic downturn along with much of her status. Many in China now see her as an "antihero" of "unbridled capitalism".[13]

Today, girls and women make up half of China's formal workforce, at some 330 million strong. However, it was only as recently as July 2008 that the first sexual harassment case was brought before the courts and won.[14] I should also note that China is the only country in the world where more women commit suicide than men—one woman kills herself there every four minutes—150,000 a year, while another 1.5 million attempt suicide.[15] Misogyny and sexual discrimination define the lives of a majority of women laborers while a few women also occupy new locations of power.

Alongside all the "newest" change in China is also the heart-breaking story of the young girl Yu Shui, with her Western name, Cindy, recorded in the documentary film, *Up the Yangtze*. She is the daughter of illiterate peasants who cannot afford to send her to college, so she suffers with her dreams while working aboard a tourist boat, homesick and displaced. The film by director Yung Chang documents the human impact of the giant Three Gorges Dam project as the Yangtze river rises and floods its land-scape, displacing 2 million ordinary Chinese from their homes. This human suffering is the other side of China's "economic miracle".

In the evening of the day I saw *Up the Yangtze*, I watched the spectacular closing ceremonies of the Chinese Olympics. Unlike the opening ceremony, which harkened back to China's past, this looked to the "harmony" of the future with its ethereal sense of possibility. I thought of Yu Shui who also must be given a chance at a future.

All the above discussion takes on its newest meanings as China suffers the global economic meltdown with the rest of the world. Its economic expansion is slowing as the global downturn reduces demand for its products. In November 2008, China's stock market lost almost half of its value. On the other side of the globe, in the US, millions continue to lose their jobs and melamine traces are found here too in infant formula, even though they are said to be present in non-hazardous amounts. The borders of China and the US continue to morph into new forms of economic porousness.

China's suggestion of and urging for a replacement of the dollar as the world's reserve currency ups the ante in new and uncharted ways. As China jockeys for a new positioning to reflect its new economic power, the globe is shifting once again.

Notes

1   James Fallows, "Interesting Times", *Atlantic Monthly*, April, 2009, pp. 54–63.

2   Michael Wines and Edward Wong, "China Takes Stage as World Economic Power, But Its Transformation Is Incomplete", *New York Times*, April 2, 2009, p. A12; and Keith Bradsher, "China Vies to Be World's Leader in Electric Cars", *New York Times*, April 2, 2009, p. A1.

3   Nicolai Ouroussoff, "In Changing Face of Beijing, a Look at the New China", *New York Times*, July 13, 2008, p. A1. Also see Ted Fishman, *China Inc.* (New York: Scribner, 2005).

4   Thomas Friedman, "A Biblical Seven Years", *New York Times*, August 27, 2008, p. A23.

5   Paul Goldberger, "Out of the Blocks", *New Yorker*, June 2, 2008, p. 71.

6   Naomi Klein, "China's All-Seeing Eye", *Rolling Stone*, May 29, 2008. www.rollingsone.com/politics/story/20797485/chinas_all seeing_eye/print

7   James Fallows, "The $1.4 Trillion Question", *The Atlantic Monthly*, January/February, 2008, p. 47.

8   Evan Osnos, "Angry Youth", *The New Yorker*, July 28, 2008, p. 29.

9   See Jacques Leslie's informative article, "The Last Empire", *Mother Jones*, vol. 33, no. 1 (January–February, 2008), pp. 30, 31, 34, 35, 83.

10 Joseph Kahn and Jim Yardley, "As China Roars, Pollution Reaches Deadly Extremes", *New York Times*, August 26, 2007, p. A1.

11 Sebastian Junger, "Enter China, the Giant", *Vanity Fair*, July, 2007, pp. 130, 138.

12 Martin Hart-Landsberg and Pual Burkett, "China, Capitalist Accumulation, and Labor", *Monthly Review*, vol. 59, no. 1 (May, 2007), p. 21.

13 Evan Osnos, "Wastepaper Queen", *New Yorker*, March 30, 2009, p. 46.

14 Megan Shank, "No Longer Silent", *Ms. Magazine*, vol. XIX, no. 1 (Winter, 2009), p. 24.

15 These are statistics from the World Health Organization. See: Lisa Movius, "Women on the Verge", *Ms. Magazine*, Summer 2007, pp. 24, 26.

New-Old Discourses on the Globe

....

8

God Bless America and Her Troops

As I introduce this discussion about secularism, let me say that I am an atheist and a non-religious Jew. I do not believe in God, or a God, which is different than saying God does not exist. S/he just does not exist for me.

There is a resurgence of religion today—political Islam, Christian conservatism, and Hindu nationalism—with the rise of the newest form of global capitalism. Capitalism, in the form of "market fundamentalism", could itself be said to be the newest religion of choice for the nation state in global flux. Despite the horrific effects of the global economic meltdown, capitalism remains unscathed as the preferred system of those who dominate it.

US politicians today fall all over themselves declaring their commitment to religious faith. They are at the ready to tell us of their religiosity; how God is part of their lives; how their faith instructs them and informs their ethics. The controversy surrounding Reverend Wright's remarks and relationship to Obama during the presidential campaign was painful and costly for Obama, but nevertheless established Obama as a religious man. He needed this religiosity to be a viable candidate even if the black church seemed a bit too angry for most white Americans. Reverend Wright did not say much that is different than what Martin Luther King said, but times have changed, and Wright's words, "God damn America" were heard differently, and angrily. King had a dream, Obama has hope, and Wright was a nightmare.

It is significant that the Western, "modern" world distinguishes itself from "others" across the globe as being self-proclaimedly secular and rational, and not religious and fanatical. Religion in the West is of another type and order than Islam. Islamophobia is actually constructed from the equation between religious radicalism and irrational governing. In today's depiction of Islam the middle ground of rationality alongside and with religion drops off the map.

As I attempt to realign the interdependent relationship between secularity and religiosity let me clarify that I think there are salient and real differences between the theocratic state and the secular one. Yet the secular state is never and has never been secular enough. Although the oneness of political rule in a theocratic state is always oppressive and repressive to the diversity of religions, and to the interpretations of any one religious doctrine, the pluralism of secularity is and never has been fully radical and inclusive. Therefore, the overdrawn dichotomy between West and East, or secular and religious, inhibits radically democratic discourses for this historical moment.

Religions, like races, shift and change. Their location in the world of politics always needs context. According to Talal Asad, secularism arose in modern Euro-America and is closely allied with the modern nation state, which is supposed to be independent and autonomous of religion, and of its violent wars. Secularism transcends individual differing religions and as such is assumed to be free of religious warfare. Asad argues, however, that secularism shifted the violence of religious wars to the violence of the nationalist and colonialist state. Secularism arose with the capitalist nation state and defends it with a new violence and intolerance. Both the religious and the secular state are constantly being remade, and simple opposition does not adequately explain their relationship to each other.[1]

Horrific cruelty has been done under the auspices of secular states. One need only quickly glance at the imperial wars in Afghanistan and Iraq. President Bush officiated in a secular state while all the while invoking God as part of his war-making decision process. Under Bush/Cheney the US authorized torture for secular/democratic good. In addition, the European conquest of Africa and of Asia; Nazi Germany; Stalin's Russia; imperial Japan; the Khmer Rouge; Mao's China, were all secular, so to speak.[2] This is not to absolve religious tyrannical rule whenever and wherever it exists, but rather to query the opposition of secularity and religiosity on the basis of rationality and violence.

According to Gil Anidjar, secularism too often stands in for "universal reason". Instead, he argues that neither category—secular nor religious—is fixed and that too often "secular is a mask for religion" while other times they define and depend on each other for their meaning and obscure each other while doing so. In this sense, Christianity becomes a façade while inventing the distinction between the religious and the secular. By inventing this distinction between religion and secularism, Christianity made religion the problem, rather than itself. They function together as foils, as "devices for obfuscation and self-blinding". More simply put, "secularism is a name Christianity gave itself when it invented religion, when it named its other or others as religious".[3]

In this argument, Christianity parades silently while Islam is made the fanatical religion. Religious people are not Christian in similar ways to the way people of color are made "not white". The silence of privilege neutralizes and normalizes Christianity as though it were universal and rational. For Asad, this parallels the way the language of human rights and international law became part of the "new civilizing mission" aimed at the Orient. Religion is located in the Orient, "the imperial realm to be governed and dominated, bombed, reformed and civilized". In a tour de force of interpreting Edward Said Anidjar writes: "Secularism is Orientalism: And Orientalism is Christianity. It is Christian imperialism".[4]

I wish to use this notion of secularism as deeply embedded in religiosity without losing the specificities of difference that exist within differing religious and secular histories. I do not dismiss the huge importance of secular politics in democratic politics but also believe that most often secular politics has not been sufficiently radically pluralistic. It is also important to note that not all religious beliefs function cruelly and exclusively.

African American churches fought hard for the rights of US blacks and others against poverty and economic humiliation. And political struggles identified as secular demands for human and women's rights have had enormous impact on improving people's lives. Yet, the US empire has used religiosity to authorize *irrational* wars. The silencing of religiosity within secularism needs exposure, and un-silencing. Secular states must cleanse themselves of their exclusionary religiosity.

During the 2008 presidential election Obama presented himself as a deeply religious person, and for him this meant he was Christian. I thought he too readily rejected the identity of Muslim when it was assigned him. He often went to great lengths to make clear that he was not Muslim, given that his father was, when he was "accused" of being so. I often wished that he would at least clarify that there is no problem with being Muslim, even if he is not. But he never did. His continual denials left Christianity as his preferred status.

Obama openly embraced and supported the idea of renewing faith-based initiatives for dealing with present social problems. He had already found such initiatives successful in his experience in Chicago and would use that as a partial model. By claiming churches as a location for this work he also became more Christian, and therefore less Muslim. As such, he remains secular, though religious, because he is Christian, and not Muslim. By coding non-Christian religions as "religion", Christianity disguises itself as secularism. Obama distanced himself from his father's Islam and instead embraced his mother's Christianity. When he finally broke with Reverend Wright, he could do so without looking un-Christian.

Obama often remarked during the campaign that "we worship an awesome God in the blue states". He also made clear his belief that religiosity in the public sphere is not always a problem. "Not every mention of God in public is a breach to the wall of separation." As well, speaking to a group of secularists, he said that it is wrong to "ask believers to leave their religion at the door before entering into the public square". He argued for a "sense of proportion" in guiding those who "police the boundaries between church and state".[5] It would seem that Obama's victory may have been a win for secular Christianity, and a loss, at least for now, for extreme Evangelical/Pentecostal Christianity.

Yet his choice of the Evangelical Rick Warren as the pastor for the inauguration called for more than a simple skepticism. Warren is known to be against both civil rights of marriage for gays and abortion rights for women. Obama defended his choice of Warren, citing the need to build a big tent for us all. Yet by the time inauguration day rolled around the tent had been happily stretched even further. Obama welcomed all religions, including, for a first time, naming Muslims. And he recognized the rights of non-believers as well. I remember hearing Obama mention non-believers, and thinking that this meant me. I am pretty sure that this particular inclusion is a first for a US president.

It is also quite hopeful that Obama granted his first White House interview upon becoming president to the Arab Dubai-based satellite TV channel Al Arabiya and openly embraced a dialogue with the Muslim world, especially to address the crisis situation between Israelis and Palestinians as well as Iran. Similar to his inaugural address, he described the US as a country of Christians, Muslims, Jews, *and* non-believers. He noted that he has Muslims in his family and has lived in and traveled in Muslim countries. He directed US envoy George Mitchell to listen, much like Achebe advises, rather than to speak in monologue, to find a bridge for peace in the Middle East.

In stark contrast George Bush during his right-wing religious presidency spoke openly of being a born-again Christian and having been "saved" from his former alcoholic self. He won 78 percent of the white Evangelical vote in each of his elections. These same right-wing Evangelicals who supported Bush continue to try and hold the Republican Party hostage to their conservative and punishing agendas.

Senator McCain's choice of Sarah Palin for his vice-presidential running mate was in part caused by this pressure. McCain was judged not right wing enough for the Evangelical ideologues in his party who are committed to archaic laws for women and gays. This Evangelical singular focus against abortion and assault on human rights via the Supreme Court welcomed and ushered in Palin's demagoguery.

Her positions on abortion, domestic partner benefits, sexual abstinence, creationism, and stem cell research were all at one with the right-wing ideologues'. She was a perfect fit: gun-toting, anti-taxing, and full of populist resentment. She was just too good to be true—"a walking advertisement for 'pro-life' policies". And, somewhat unexpectedly, "she thrilled the women in their churches". She tapped into a huge reservoir of angst among these struggling moms of the "conservative independent sisterhood".[6] Pentecostal Palin stood for white women's uplift. Her credentials touted no pedigree, earned or not. She symbolized modernity fused with the inspirited world—a governor with five kids.

Palin's religious stance did not promise much for her foreign policy expertise. Many Pentecostals believe that "spiritual warfare between godly and satanic forces underlies all earthly conflicts" and that the Iraq war is an expression of this. Frances Fitzgerald was not hopeful. Palin has "spent much more time in church than she has foreign policy and the habit of mind these churches instill has little to do with diplomacy or peacemaking".[7] The war in Iraq, for Palin, "is a task that is from God".[8]

The religious complexity of Christianity in the US should not go unnoticed. As much as one quarter of its population identifies as Evangelical, and many of them are right-wing conservatives.

And, yet it would be wrong not to also recognize that there is a growing progressive part of the Evangelical movement. Many of these voters—as much as one third of them—voted Democratic in 2008 and also did so for Bill Clinton in 1992 and 1996. These Evangelicals want to curb global warming, provide debt relief for poor countries, support a comprehensive immigration reform bill, wish for an end to the war in Iraq, and are committed to addressing poverty and human rights issues. They lack the virulent stance of the culture wars and wish to provide what they believe is a "consistent pro-life agenda", rather than a simplistic anti-abortion doctrine.[9]

The political struggles and wars over religion and with religion need serious attention. The entire globe begs for a way to embrace creative thinking about the secular/religious divide. Religious and atheistic beliefs must both find a radically democratic embrace of people's equality *and* freedom. There is no inherent conflict and opposition between those who believe in a God, and those who do not. Secularism must move beyond its Christianity, while other religious nationalisms and theocracies must recognize and embrace the democratic tenets embedded in their religiosity.

Today, this road to discovery may be found among Muslim women struggling against theocracy and defiantly attempting to re-interpret the Koran for its democratic meanings. This may possibly be a more hopeful location than the Christian nationalist demagoguery and totalitarianism sometimes found in the US and Africa alike.[10] So I will continue to look for the newest dialogues by and among believing and non-believing Muslim women who are searching for the radically egalitarian meanings of democracy.

Notes

1   Talal Asad, *Formations of the Secular: Christianity, Islam, Modernity* (Stanford: Stanford University Press, 2003), pp. 1, 2, 6, 7, 99, 100.

2   Ibid., p. 101.

3   Gil Anidjar, "Secularism", *Critical Inquiry*, 33 (Autumn, 2006), pp. 57, 62, 63. Also see: Jacques Derrida, ed. and introduced by Gil Anidjar, *Acts of Religion* (New York: Routledge, 2002).

4   Ibid., "Secularism", pp. 65, 66.

5   Peter J. Boyer, "Party Faithful", *New Yorker*, September 8, 2008, p. 28.

6   Frances Fitzgerald, "A Fateful Election", *New York Review of Books*, vol. LV, no. 17 (November 6, 2008), p. 12.

7   Ibid.

8   David Martin, "Have Pentecostalism, Will Travel", *The Times Literary Supplement*, September 17, 2008, p. 10.

9   Frances Fitzgerald, "The New Evangelicals", *The New Yorker*, June 30, 2008, pp., 27, 29.

10 Michelle Goldberg, *Kingdom Coming* (New York: Norton, 2006), pp. 23, 107.

9

New Cold Wars and Global Warming

The Cold War ended, in a fashion, with the revolutions of 1989 and the fall of the Soviet empire. Fears about nuclear war then became part of anti-terrorism rather than anti-communism.

Despite this shift, in fall 2008 there was much noise about a new imperial Russia that needed to be reckoned with. Enter our presidential campaign. Vote for John McCain and he would keep the US safe from another Cold War. McCain was prepared to stand firmly against Russian prime minister Vladimir Putin as the aggressor during Georgian president Mikheil Saakashvili's attempt to retake South Ossetia. Sarah Palin even suggested that the US might have to go to war with Russia in order to protect Georgia.[1] Then president Bush also sided with Georgia's president Saakashvili, calling Russia the aggressor. Old rhetoric was used to mobilize anti-communist positionings when they made no new sense. The longstanding politics of oil, and the need to maintain safe corridors for its delivery, were behind the rhetoric.

According to Michael Klare, the Caspian Sea basin houses the leading energy providers, and these providers are all former socialist republics of the Soviet Union. The Republic of Georgia maintains an energy corridor for the export of this oil to the West. At the heart of this newest Georgian–Russian confrontation was Moscow's desire to control this oil. The US has deep investments in Georgia to hold on to the control of this flow. Putin was at the ready, and vied openly in this contestation over the supply of oil.[2]

To begin with, it may not be all that accurate to think of the period pre-1989 as a cold war. Mahmood Mamdani has made the case that there were "hot" wars going on all over the world during this time. Although there was peace in the two key empires that defined this period, there was little peace to be found elsewhere.[3] Mamdani also argues that the imperial powers of neocolonial domination continue to define and control the meanings of war and genocide today. He points to the International Criminal Court (ICC) as the latest location for seeing the distortion of Africa's history, especially in Darfur. "We have the astonishing spectacle of the state that has perpetrated the violence in Iraq, the United States, branding an adversary state, Sudan, the one that has perpetrated genocidal violence in Darfur. Even more astonishing, we had a citizens' movement in America calling for a humanitarian intervention in Darfur while keeping mum about the violence in Iraq."[4] Mamdani calls for vigilance in identifying the privileged viewpoints from which the world is named and, therefore, understood.

Similar querying must be done to identify the vested interests that shape discussion of the financial crisis of Wall Street. To whose benefit is it that the US taxpayer should shore up failing mortgages and US banks? The bailout started as an $800 billion —and counting—extravaganza of US finance capitalists. The post-communist "triumph" of capitalism appears to need a new face.

Republican spokespeople, and former presidential nominee Mitt Romney, argued that the best thing for the failed auto companies was to declare bankruptcy and then streamline and downsize wages, pensions, and health care. Romney said this was the way the auto companies would regain solvency and a competitive edge. Obama has more recently embraced this position. A bit of Soviet "workers' rights" rhetoric might not be a bad thing here.

US political rhetoric celebrates the supposed triumph of freedom and democracy—whether in the collapse of the Soviet Union, or the supposed reconstruction of Iraq. Contradictorily, democracy is destroyed at home.[5] The US political class moved from its "free market fundamentalist" rhetoric to handing out bailouts with no gun fired. Billions of dollars were transferred from US taxpayers to US banks. US taxpayers were told that they must give the treasury over to the crooks that have profited from their selfish acts.

This silent revolution resembles other neoliberal takeovers of the past. In 1989, while the Soviet Union was collapsing, so was affirmative action law and the liberal democratic legal order in the US. And yet again, the Cheney-led destruction of neoliberal rights after September 11, 2001, was authorized by the silent triumph of the US "terror-state".

McCain ran for president, and lost using too much old "free market" rhetoric while the devastatingly new economic crisis loomed large. He was caught in the past, his past, of Vietnam and the old Cold War, and his past and present support of the war in Iraq. When all else was failing McCain drew on his POW experience: he was tough, and patriotic, and he loved his country. He was marketed as a war hero in Cold War fashion despite the fact that his war broke him, and the US lost it.[6] His support for the Iraq war seemed only to underscore his ties to the past. McCain was out of touch, and out of date. The fact that he spoke as a veteran and had done little to support the needs of returning Afghan and Iraq war veterans, especially the thousands who are disabled and in need of extended medical care, did not help his case.

Vietnam and the Cold War remain echoes in an unfinished global conversation. And the echo reverberated when McCain implored the American public to finish the war in Iraq with honor—as though war can "solve otherwise insoluble problems".[7] It was key to Obama's campaign that he would draw down troops and end the war in Iraq and refocus on Afghanistan.

Obama, once becoming president, has reassigned troops to Afghanistan even though more Americans have already been killed there than in the first nine years of the Vietnam War, 1956–64.[8] It needs to be remembered that the Afghan war, in part, brought the Soviet empire to its knees while it also put the US in bed with the "anti-communist" Taliban. Whispers of Cold War politics remain.

It is of little surprise that the trail of oil is not too far away. Global posturing continues throughout the Middle East. In January 2007, the price of oil was less than $60 a barrel. By summer 2008 it had hit a new record of $147. Then, for the first time ever, people in the US paid up to four dollars a gallon for gasolene. By January 2009 oil profits along with much else in the global economy had bottomed out. Wars over oil continue apace. They are made and remade.

The newest concerns with oil supply have become more complicated because they exist alongside the need for arable land, clean water, and safe environments. The newest demands of global capitalism require more of everything when there is less of everything. Less land and water is available, to sustain these new needs. The continual search for oil should be constrained by these environmental concerns, but it is not.

At home, Palin's petropolitics as governor of Alaska increased income from gas production with little regard for the environment and alternative energies. As mentioned earlier, Alaska has no state income tax—oil revenues replaced the need for taxation as a source of revenue. As oil revenues drop, Alaska's existing policies are jeopardized.

In 2007 Alaska produced approximately 719,000 barrels of oil a day, which put it in a similar position with Egypt and Malaysia. But environmentalists warn that this continued production puts Alaska's environmental integrity at risk. Michael Klare warns that the inevitable decrease in global oil output, alongside the fact that global warming is an inescapable truth, means that the environment is at greater risk in Alaska than elsewhere.[9]

Global warming demands new visions that stand against the excessive greed and selfishness of unbridled market fundamentalism. Echoes of the Cold War that misrepresent the choices for poor people across the globe must be quieted while the complex interdependencies of our planet are recognized and embraced. Al Gore presented his film *Inconvenient Truth* as a small, even if inadequate, beginning in this process.

Gore's message is that the planet's situation is dire. His film, set as a PowerPoint lecture, tells the story of global warming. The planet is heating up — the result is that glaciers are melting, oceans are rising, and lakes are evaporating; heavy rains and hurricanes are caused by the warming trends of the oceans. Given these warming trends, mosquitoes can live at higher altitudes above the mosquito line, invasive transplants replace native plants, asthma is worse, and so forth. He ends with a plea that people must act now.

The film is also about Gore. That he has been committed to reversing these trends for the past thirty years. That personal tragedy—his son's devastating car accident and Gore's sister's death to lung cancer—has underscored the need to take action and not just limp along. He uses his personal story to create a political narrative, and although some say this is self-serving I rather think that it is astute. As most feminists would argue, one's personal life informs one's political commitments.

Gore argues that there is plenty of evidence that documents the trend of global warming. His film carefully confirms this reality, and the Academy of Science issued a report confirming the facts. Many scientists endorsed the film as one way of impugning the Bush administration's unconscionable denial of these trends. The difficulty is taking Gore's message of catastrophe and mapping a plan to reverse it. The problem seems almost too big to solve. Gore is proof that a new political strategy is needed. After all, he tells us that he spoke on global warming in governmental hearings for years and throughout the Clinton administration. Talk is clearly not enough.

The audience where I saw the film was very energized to do their part. In a discussion afterwards people offered their individual willingness to do more: to remember to turn off lights and conserve energy, to install solar power when possible, to buy a hybrid car. But none of this is sufficient, or even possible for many, even if it is necessary. Political mobilization that focuses on a set of environmental demands that the US, along with the rest of the globe, must adhere to is needed. And this will demand a radical critique of the endless excessive greed of global capital.

There is a growing movement across the globe to support "green" jobs that will help create needed work for people, while respecting the needs of the planet. According to Van Jones, global warming and urban poverty must be recognized as two sides of the same coin: "green jobs—weatherizing buildings, installing solar panels, and constructing mass transit systems"—should go to the poor and unemployed. He believes that "the green economy should not be just about reclaiming thrown-away stuff. It should be about reclaiming thrown-away communities".[10]

There are women's movements in Kenya, South Africa, and Ghana to name a few that are planting trees and trying to reverse climate change. They are organizing and demanding a different world. If the planet is to get a hold of it's deteriorating environmental state, radical listening to these voices is needed.

Instead of privatized bailouts the globe needs a resurgence of publicly focused interventions. Make it illegal for auto companies to produce non-energy-efficient automobiles. Build public transportation for people across the US and the globe and require its use. End war making, which only creates more and more carbon emissions and heat. Develop renewable sources of energy not dependent on carbons, such as wind, tides, and maybe safe nuclear power. Treat the production of carbon dioxide as production of a pollutant.

Global warming demands an end to all wars, hot and cold, now. Global warming requires an end to the excessive need for oil and with it militarized capitalism. And it begs for protection for our forests, and oceans, and rivers, and mangroves, so tsunamis and hurricanes do not continue to devastate us all.

Notes

1   Mark Ames and Ari Berman, "McCain's Kremlin Ties", *The Nation*, vol. 287, no. 12 (October 20, 2008), pp. 19, 20.

2   Michael Klare, "Putin's Ruthless Gambit; The Bush Administration Falters in a Geopolitical Chess Match", www.potside.org/archive. Also see his *Rising Powers, Shrinking Planet* (New York: Metropolitan Books, 2008).

3   Mahmood Mamdani, *Good Muslim, Bad Muslim* (New York: Pantheon Books, 2004), pp. 90–98.

4   Mahmood Mamdani, "The New Humanitarian Order", *The Nation*, vol. 287, no. 9 (September 29, 2008), p. 20.

5   Zillah Eisenstein, *The Color of Gender: Reimaging Democracy* (Berkeley: University of California Press, 1994), chapter 1; and *Sexual Decoys* (London: Zed Books, 2007).

6   Sydney H. Schanberg, "McCain and the POW Cover-up", *The Nation*, vol. 287, no. 10 (October 6, 2008), p. 27.

7   Jeffrey Goldberg, "The Wars of John McCain", *Atlantic Monthly*, October, 2008, p. 51.

8   Thomas Johnson and M. Chris Mason, "All Counterinsurgency is Local", *Atlantic Monthly*, October, 2008, p. 36.

9   Michael Klare, "Palin's Petropolitics", *The Nation*, vol. 287, no. 10 (October 6, 2008), pp. 4, 6.

10 Van Jones, quoted in Elizabeth Kolbert, "Greening the Ghetto", *New Yorker*, January 12, 2009, p. 25.

10

Mythic Enemies and Newest Races

When President Bush first named "the axis of evil" after September 11, 2001, he gave new life to old fears and old imperial arrogance. Iran, Afghanistan, Iraq, North Korea, and Syria became the problem to deter even if most Americans do not know where these countries are, or what their histories have been. Enemies became a smokescreen for the havoc Bush created: a national debt approaching $10 trillion; five million more people falling into poverty; an increase of seven million more without health insurance; the displacement of four and half million Iraqis; the dire wounding of over 30,000 US soldiers.

There was no end to the devastation and destruction of ordinary people's lives while Bush usurped "unitary executive" powers. He waged undeclared wars, created military courts, authorized "extraordinary renditions and secret prisons", increased coercive interrogation, established "trials with undisclosed evidence", and overrode congressional oversight on all kinds of policy.[1] With such a scenario, it helps to have "others" to fear.

North Korea is an old-type enemy of a particular kind, a leftover of the Cold War. The country is horribly poverty stricken and continually punished in and by the new global economy, but no matter, given its enemy status. North Korea is constructed as an enemy to fear, with nuclear possibilities. There is little memory, if any, that North Korea is a US-made creation from the days of staunch anti-communist Cold War politics. This era is fundamentally changed with the demise of the Soviet Union, and yet this last enemy remains.

I remember visiting Ewha Women's University in South Korea and realizing that most South and North Koreans see themselves as split families, not as two countries, let alone enemies. Bush's demonizing rhetoric about the North's latest threats related to nuclear testing was at a height while I was lecturing at Ewha. Most of the people I spoke with on this visit pleaded for a more sane US policy. They did not accept the "enemy" status of part of their nation, nor could they understand the demonizing of the North.

Ewha University is the largest women's university in the world with over 20,000 female students. In the morning when classes are to begin, a sea of women trudge out from the underground subway on their way from home to school. The first day I was there it looked to me like a massive feminist demonstration. Why else would so many women be out and about together? It was amazing to view these thousands of young women walking quickly with books in hand, chatting with friends, moving towards the campus.

While in Seoul, I stayed in the university's guest room and ate my meals in the cafeteria. I had miso soup and kimchee for breakfast. Most of the girls chose the American breakfast— cereal and a bun. They seemed so much like my own students in their attire and presentation of themselves. They could not fathom the US hatred toward the North.

Korean feminisms are very committed to peace activism and anti-militarism, and the "reunification of Korea". As such they disallow the easy "enemy status" construction. As a result, little is heard about these feminisms in the US. These feminisms are critical of patriarchal privilege, gendered colonialism, and traditional Confucianism, although they remain in critical dialogue with each. They struggle for a non-essentialized collectivity that denies over-universalized gender truths, while still often being bound by the status quo. But as they dislodge overdrawn notions of women's shared experience, they call forth their own racialized experiences of gender. There are beginnings of an anti-racist feminism with global roots — and routes — that is all too often unrecognized as such.[2]

Old enemies are never sufficient, especially when the dialogue, as in the case of North Korea, is obviously outdated and over-blown. New enemies are in the process of being identified in newer, updated fashion. Bush/Cheney were obsessed with their anti-terrorist/anti-radical Islam rhetoric when they mobilized against Iraq and later Iran. These newest enemy sites travel and shift and morph while there is a renewing of the rhetoric of the war of/on "terror" new locations. The war on/of "terror" that began with Afghanistan, then shifted to Iraq, and then to Iran, has now shifted back towards Afghanistan, and Pakistan, once again.

Obama vows to take the fight against terrorism to its supposed stronghold in both Afghanistan and Pakistan. It is more than troubling to think about what this might mean. Afghanistan has been decimated by war since the Cold War and the 1950s. When the US began its bombing in 2001, Afghanistan's rich history and culture were already under siege and in shambles. By the summer of 2008, it was repeatedly stated in US presidential election rhetoric that the Taliban had gained a toehold again with a new mobilization, and needed to be countered.

It is lesser known that much of the Taliban's activity and resurgence were in large part in response to increased US bombing at that time. According to John Pilger, an estimated 1,853 bombs have been dropped — the 500-pound and 2,000-pound satellite-guided kind during 2008.[3] Even quiescent Afghan president Hamid Karzai said that the Taliban's aggression was in reaction to US policy, which was fueling the warlords. And, the Taliban is not one unified political force to begin with, but represents varied right-wing Islamic tendencies.

The manufacture of enemies always requires historical amnesia and repetitive distortions. Iran, which was defined in and by the Persian Empire, stood at and as the global center of cultural and historical life in the seventh century. Muslim greatness at this time was distinctly Persian. In the Babylonian period, Jewish Iranians were Persian.

Today Iran remains in part Persian, in part Islamic, and in part Western. Its culture has porous borders. Persia and Islam should not be reduced to the same entity because they are unique identities, although often blended. Persia was the world's first superpower, and was today's Iraq, Pakistan, Afghanistan, Turkmenistan, Turkey, Lebanon, Syria, Egypt, and Israel. Iran, which is so often wrongly equated with the Islamic threat, is Persian, and mainly Shiite, not Arab Sunni.[4] Shiites in Iran and Iraq form deep ties and loyalties that the US has yet to recognize or understand.

Neither the recent past, nor the present, is ever sufficient to allow comprehensive knowledge or understanding of a country and its history. Iran has a strong tradition of democratic theory, even if it is not always recognizable in the US because of its other-than-Western forms, or because of its more recent transitions. Democracies must be seen in their plural formulations and histories, rather than their overly homogenized "othered" positionings.[5] And one should not forget the Bush/Cheney legacy as they think about what should be considered democratic in the first place.

In present-day rhetoric, democracy, and with it global capital, are most often tied to secular societies, and religiosity to non/undemocratic ones. But, according to Hamid Dabashi and Gil Anidjar, Christianity often disguises itself as secularism, and then other non-Christian religions become the heart of the secular problem for democracy.[6] As such, Iran is very often demonized as fanatically religious, and not secular and democratic. However, if Iran as Islamic were not seen as the opposite of the West then Islam could be viewed as a major faith of global communities, instead of as the mythic enemy.[7]

As Iran has blended with global markets its middle class has grown, and reform movements have taken hold. Through the

1950s, Ali Shariati mobilized the youth, and the revolutionary fervor of what he termed freedom fighters rather than holy warriors. This led the way to the Islamic Revolution of 1979, overthrowing the Western-supported Shah Pahlavi, and establishing a Shiite theocracy with Ayatollah Khomeini.

The revolution was a keen disappointment to many progressive Iranians. It became too theocratic, even if it was a necessary and crucial break with the past. Feelings about the revolution remain complex and ambivalent among its supporters. Changes resulting from the revolution have been complicated to assess, with moderating trends as well as new extremisms. There was a liberalization finally with Mohammad Khatami, 1997–2005.[8] Yet today the fanaticism of Ahmadinejad smothers much of this democratic struggle.

Given the othering of Iran there has been little recognition of Iranian feminisms and the struggles for democracy initiated by women's human rights activist groups. There were early beginnings of these struggles in 1934, and again in 1941, and 1953.[9] Today a more-than-year-long initiative is underway— called the One Million Signatures Campaign—to help reform discriminatory laws towards women. In 2007, out of the 264 seats available on councils in provincial capitals, 44 went to women. Iranian women are actively seeking their rights as women.[10] Initiatives such as these are ignored by political brokers in the West.

Migrants and displaced persons seek safe haven from the perpetual wars of/against "terror" on this globe; they look for work in a world that continually makes access to a livelihood more elusive. Muslims and Arabs migrate toward France, Holland, Britain, and Australia. These fast-growing populations define the newest developments of Eurabia. Cultural conflict, and struggles for recognition and human rights, define the present in Iran, Pakistan, the Middle East, and so on.

Newly new zones of poverty are created alongside new riches. An estimated 1,200,000 or more refugees from Iraq live in

Jordan and Syria, and tens of thousands of refugees from Afghanistan subsist in Pakistan and Iran. Europe and North America have known little of these consequences. The UN Fund for Population estimates that there were 200 million immigrants in the world in 2006, half of them women. It also finds that 190 million people across the globe are foreign-born (meaning born outside their country of permanent residence)—which is 3 percent of the world's population.

In North America this percentage is 13 percent. Depending on one's location and one's needs, Europe and North America become places of hope and promise, or closed fortresses. One is or becomes legal or illegal. Life becomes more insecure and worrisome in the transnational globe. "Capital is exported, while workers and the poor are deported."[11]

These forced and chosen movements of people realign national and cultural identities with specific economic complexities. Differences are exacerbated as life becomes more fragile. Present-day conflicts deny and misrepresent important histories that would otherwise allow a common humanity that unites Asia, Europe, Africa, South America and the United States. A newest enemy becomes "the" Muslim while China and India become the newest successes of the globe, even if not democratic enough.

New constructions of nations and races are continuously manufactured to assist in the "othering" process that allows for the creation of necessary enemies. As the Nigerian Pius Adesanmi states: "Christianity manufactured the unbeliever; Islam, the infidel; America, the nigger; Germany, the jew; Afrikaners, the kaffir, and so on …"[12] The erasure of the Chinese holocaust at Nanking during World War Two disallows a camaraderie of anti-fascist forces and instead leaves racial borders in place. And the fact that the walking-dead of Auschwitz called themselves "Muselmann", which translates as "Muslim", is seldom made part of a historically complex connection between Muslim and Jew. Racialized borders that are porous are instead presented as rigid and unchanged. Racialized enemies are harbored here: in the made-up stories of militarized histories.

While the Chinese triumphed at the 2008 Olympics and appeared to be the new benefactors of the global economy I watched Ang Lee's film, *Lust/Caution*, which quietly hints towards the rape of Nanking and the Japanese destruction and occupation of the city. This most often forgotten and ignored Asian history of World War Two draws attention to the 1937 massacre in which at least 340,000 Chinese civilians were killed, defiled and bayoneted, and another 80,000 women were raped, mutilated and killed.[13] Alongside this atrocity many Japanese themselves were victims of Japan's aggressive war.

Over 1.5 million Japanese soldiers were killed or wounded in battle in China, and then thousands of civilians were burned alive in Hiroshima and Nagasaki.[14] These horrors are silenced by singular phrases like "the" Holocaust. Too often this designation applies exclusively to Jews when so many others also suffered. In spite of the apparent uniformity of "race" invoked by racial hatreds, allegedly homogenous racial categories include wide swathes of differing humanity, who in turn give birth to ever more mixed and heterogenous "races". This has to be remembered if old and ignorant hatreds are not to be reproduced.

These creations of races take curious turns. I stumbled upon Gil Anidjar's revelation of the usage by Auschwitz concentration camp inmates themselves of the untranslated German word *Muselmann*, in the plural *Muselmänner*, meaning "Muslims", to describe the listless, docile, walking-dead Jews in Auschwitz. Anidjar reveals this "distinct but indissociable" relationship between Arab and Jew in his attempt to show how "the enemies of Europe are also the enemies of each other". He argues that these are "undoubtedly arbitrary names". So the Jew of the concentration camps who is already the living dead, as in deadened toward life, is associated with the Muslim, one who "submits to the will of God" and is "crouched in prayer". Seeing the walking-dead Jews of Auschwitz from afar, they look like Arabs in prayer. But the Muslim is not really seen here at all. As such, the Muslim is made invisible, and silent and unreadable. Muslims are "invisible yet everywhere", as also the Jew.[15]

The classic construction of "the" Muslim derives from the divide from Hinduism. This opposition was given renewed life with the partition of India, as Hindu, from Pakistan, as Muslim. Yet the divide smothers the multiple flows and identities that deny this partition. In *Bengal Divided*, Joya Chatterji asks for a different reading of Indian history that recognizes the role of Hindus in demanding a communalist national identity that demanded separation. According to Chatterji, wealthy *bhadralok* (the Bengali term for members of the middle class) were fearful of losing power to Muslims in Bengal and therefore fought for a separate nation for Hindus. There was no homogeneity of Hindu Bengal, and Hindus fought for their religious identity and economic privilege with their own form of communalism. Hindus were not simply secularist and nationalist in this sense. As such, the *bhadralok* Hindus were fighting against what they saw as "the despotism of Muslims" and used British rule to do so.[16]

On the one hand the globe embraces the cultural varieties it expresses. There is endless talk of religions, and yoga, and Eastern ways. Barack Obama's colored flesh appears more like the rest of the globe than the skin of a white North American. Yet there are also the cartoons, whether of Obama depicted as a Muslim, or the Prophet Muhammad with a bomb as a hat. The cartoon of the Prophet, first published in Denmark, was meant as public humiliation of a kind equating Islam with extremism and terrorism.

The variations of racialization are continuous. Ella Shohat argues that although Zionism claims to be a liberation movement for *all* Jews, Zionism as it is practiced privileges European Jews, while discriminating against Jews from Arab and Muslim countries. European Jews, the Ashkenazim, are accepted while

Arab Sephardis are muffled and silenced. This differentiation allows Israel to limit its "Easternness" and "Third Worldness".[17] Sephardi Jews were pressured to choose between an "anti-Zionist 'Arabness' and a pro-Zionist 'Jewishness'". Shoat is an Iraqi Jew. Not many in the US consider such an identity given the racialized construction of the enemies list. The continual re-racing of the globe must be separated from an enemies list of and for war and militarism.

Maybe the people of the globe will come to reject these hatreds, now that the tragic flaws of the global economy become more visible and punishing for more and more people. Maybe this revelation is why the globe rejoiced that Barack Obama won the presidency of imperial America. His race is and will be re-raced, de-raced, and maybe eventually e-rased.

Notes

1   Gary Wills, "A Fateful Election", *New York Review of Books*. Vol. LV, no. 17 (November 6, 2008), p. 16.

2   Jung-Hwa Oh, ed., *Feminist Cultural Politics in Korea* (Seoul, Korea: Prunsasang, 2005). Also see multiple articles in the *Asian Journal of Women's Studies*, published quarterly by Ewha Women's University Press since 1995.

3   John Pilger, "Obama, the Prince of Bait and Switch", *New Statesman*, July 24, 2008, p.4. and at www.JohnPilger.com.

4   Marguerite del Giudice, "Persia: Ancient Soul of Iran", *National Geographic* (August, 2008), pp. 42, 46, 48, 49.

5   Arshin Adib-Moghaddam, *Iran in World Politics: The Question of the Islamic Republic* (New York: Columbia University Press, 2008), pp. 48, 49.

6   Hamid Dabashi, *Theology of Discontent* (New Brunswick: Transaction Publishers, 1951, 2006), and his *Islamic Liberation Theology* (New York: Routledge, 2008); and Gil Anidjar, "Secularism", *Critical Inquiry*, 33 (Autumn, 2006), pp. 52–77.

7   Dabashi, *Islamic Liberation Theology*, pp. 2, 60.

8   S. M. A. Sayeed, *Iran, Before and After Khomeini* (Karachi, Pakistan, 1999).

9   Ervand Abrahamian, *Iran Between Two Revolutions* (Princeton: Princeton University Press, 1982), p. 427.

10 Arshin Adib-Moghaddam, *Iran in World Politics*, p. 160.

11 Information is culled from Darko Suvin, "Immigration: Immigration in Europe today: Apartheid or Civil Cohabitation?", *Critical Inquiry*, vol. 50, nos. 1–2 (2008), pp. 206–33.

12 Pius Adesanmi, as quoted in Obioma Nnaemeka, "Racialization and the Colonial Architecture: Othering and the Order of Things", *PMLA*, vol. 123, no. 5 (October 2008), pp. 1740–1751.

13 James Yin and Shi Young, *The Rape of Nanking: An Undeniable History in Photographs* (Chicago: Innovative Publishing Groups, 1996), p. 186. Also see: Joshua Fogel, ed., *The Nanjing Massacre in History and Historiography* (Berkeley: University of California Press, 2000); and Iris Chang, *The Rape of Nanking: The Forgotten Holocaust of WW II* (New York: Basic Books, 1997).

14 Xu Zhigeng, *Lest We Forget: Nanjing Massacre, 1937* (Beijing Chinese Literature Press, 1995), p. 12.

15 Gil Anidjar, *The Jew, the Arab, A History of the Enemy* (Stanford: Stanford University Press, 2003), pp. xxv, 44, 45, 140–147. Also see: Giorgio Agamben, *Remnants of Auschwitz* (New York: Zone Books, 2002).

16 Joya Chatterji, *Bengal Divided* (London: Cambridge University Press, 1994), pp. 28, 268.

17 Ella Shohat, "Sephardim in Israel: Zionism from the Standpoint of Its Jewish Victims", *Social Text*, no. 19/20 (Autumn, 1988), pp. 1, 2, 8, 10, 11.

US Presidential
Election Talk

11

Hillary Chose Not To Be a Feminist

Hillary and I are almost identical in age. I was a political theory graduate student while she was going to law school. I began teaching and writing while active in the women's liberation movement when Hillary was becoming a lawyer, assisting Bill to become governor. Feminists in the seventies and eighties were critiquing the patriarchal, racial and class forms of our oppression and exploitation—while Hillary was becoming a politician's wife. None of this is inherently mutually exclusive and yet it has often been so. My point is simple: Hillary could have been part of the feminist movement of her day, and chose not to be.

This comparison is meant to call attention to the contextual choices that Hillary has made. It is also about how constructs of gender shift and morph and also become outmoded. Hillary is proof that gender does not stand still—she is not the same woman or politician that she was in 1992, or the start of the 2007 primary season, or at its end in 2008. This may be all to the good, or not. That has yet to be seen. But first there is something to be learned by looking backwards, not to entrap Hillary in her past, but to see and know how gender is reformulated in and for particular political moments.

Hillary is paraded as too liberal and too feminist—by both the left and the right—when she is neither, especially in comparison to contemporaries, both then and now. She said she would not have voted for the Iraq war if she had had all the information she has now, then. But this presumes that criticism of the war wasn't really possible then, like it is now. What about US Representative Barbara Lee's vote against the war? How come Barbara Lee knew to vote against it? And why wasn't Hillary a feminist activist of the sort that her supporters in 2008 act like she was?

Hillary has a female body, but do not simply confuse this with a progressive or feminist agenda.[1] She is more often than not depicted as deeply committed to sexual and racial equality, and to a richly democratic politics that would follow from this. But, she ran a presidential primary campaign greatly at odds with this depiction. So it is important to try and tease out Hillary's actual record from the political misrepresentation and fantasy that often surround her. This concern becomes even more important when I later discuss Sarah Palin's vice-presidential candidacy. Let me explain.

I do not think it is fair to be critical of Hillary because I expect more from women than I expect from men in politics. I do not believe, in an essentialist fashion, that females or women are kinder, or gentler, or more peace-loving than men. Distinguishing here between females and women draws out an important relationship between sex and gender. Female bodies—in their biological sense—can have different meaning than their culturally constructed and chosen definitions of womanhood. Yet people assume that Hillary's femaleness stands for a particular kind of womanhood, however this might be defined; and her womanhood stands for females. But this is not always the case.

Hillary is a troubling symbol. Her private sexual life with Bill was publicized unfairly and yet her opportunism made it hard to fathom her choices, whatever they "really" are/were. Her private sexual life should be her own business but it isn't because public people are not allowed private lives. So her personal choices have public consequences because she is a political person. As such, she has a sexual politics that is public whether she speaks it or has chosen it, or not. Why does this all matter? Because sex is always already political, meaning power-filled, and it is not Hillary, the individual, so to speak, that makes this so.

Sexual and gender narratives define the cultural contours of Hillary with and without her assent. She has chosen a political and public life so hers is a public marriage. Her private life is public. Her female body has been publicly written on over and over again, while her sexual self and sexual desires are exposed and disciplined with her being a player, and also not. So it is hard to decipher her sexual or gender politics from the politics assigned her. Her ambition and opportunism only complicate this.

So long as Hillary abides by masculinist gender rules while remaining a symbol of and for women, and even feminism, there is much to lose for those who are committed to a peaceful planet. Hillary's sexual/gender politics is crucial to today's militarist politics because gender is used to naturalize war; and war is also gendered, and she is female. Masculinity and femininity are set as normal oppositions in this scenario. Women are supposedly peaceful and men make war. The enemy nation is feminized and the victor is re-masculinized. It is why rape policy—as a "murderous misogyny"—often exists as integral to military policy.[2] Imperial democracy has required sexual and racial repression, and gender(ing) becomes war in yet another form. Hillary has been a sometime public face for this re-gendering process.

Supposedly Hillary moved herself to the center and won her Senate seat while doing so. But this is partly wrong. She was already at the center. She did not need to move to the center from the left of the political spectrum. The Democratic Leadership Council (DLC) was already a dominant force when she and Bill were elected in 1992. They were the "new" Democrats at the start—neoliberal—not the old kind of liberal who believed in public responsibility for the health and welfare of citizens. They downsized and privatized government from the beginning. It is why Hillary's healthcare package failed, not because her policy proposals were too radical, or liberal, but because they were neither. She was a neoliberal who also happens to be female.

Hillary and Bill promised universal health care in 1992 with no success. Hillary never supported or presented a single payer plan; nor did she seriously propose curtailment of insurance profits. She received substantial contributions—more than $800,000—for her Senate campaign from insurance and pharmaceutical companies, more contributions from these companies than any other candidate except Senator Rick Santorum.[3] My point is that Hillary was never left-of-center and she moved rightward in the early 2008 primaries towards a kind of heightened masculinist militarism.

Hillary believes in women's rights and women's self-determination, but in neoliberal form. She remained silent, during Bill's administrations, at the dismantling of education and social welfare programs as well as the curtailment of abortion rights and access to them on the state level. Instead, Hillary sought "common ground" with anti-abortionists in the hope of avoiding controversy.

In the 1992 campaign Bill and Hillary disassociated themselves from the old-style Democratic politics. He proposed programs that would meet the needs of the "new world global order," while we were also told that this was the "year of the woman". That year, more women ran for Senate than ever before—and one was "even" African American. Of the final four presidential and vice-presidential candidates, two had wives who were lawyers—one of whom actually practiced. Barbara Bush, the quintessential Republican loyal wife, addressed the Republican convention whereas the Democrats kept their wives off center stage. Barbara presented herself in a homey, self-denigrating fashion and enjoyed record popularity. She used her paper-thin persona to bring in whatever pluralist vote existed for the Republicans. She became the party's umbrella.

Hillary was the other election icon. As her husband Bill pointed out, one would have thought George Herbert Walker Bush was running against her. And in some sense he was. Republicans dangled her before the public as a radical feminist, an arch critic of marriage and family, and a defender of children's rights to sue parents. All this was done in order to delegitimize the Democrats. Everyone, including Hillary, seemed to ignore the likelihood that if she had been a radical feminist, she might have run for the presidency herself.

Hillary's early outspoken role in the 1992 campaign unfolded amidst charges of her husband's infidelity. She was drawn into the Gennifer Flowers affair to defend Bill's faithfulness. Hillary appeared on TV with Bill to set the Flowers' allegations straight and said she was no "stand-by-your-man woman". But to most watching she looked like one as she tried to silence the rumors of infidelity as only a wife can do. Hillary's early active protective role on behalf of her husband was often used to depict them as forming the now infamous "co-presidency".

Political rhetoric was at high pitch then. Republicans trumpeted the traditional white patriarchal family while Democrats sported a more modern family form with educated wives. "Family values" became the Republicans' code words for anti-abortion, anti-feminist, anti-affirmative-action, anti-homosexual, anti-social-welfare, and anti-drug policies. The language of "family values" purported to be about saving America as it once was. Back then Hillary symbolized more of what the world was coming to be—a new kind of gender flexibility.

Barbara Bush was spokeswoman for the old model of supportive political wife, while Marilyn Quayle represented the newer Republican breed of professional women who defer to their wifely responsibilities. Bush and Quayle hoped that Hillary would seem too different, too modern, and too scary. And she was different from Barbara and Marilyn although she too remained dutiful to Bill, as his wife.

In this "year of the woman" women were still mainly wives, and neither party brought feminist issues to center stage. Although Hillary represented a sea change for American women, she still was bound and gagged as a political wife. She also was not very left or liberal, as already noted: she served on Wal-Mart's board of directors and remained silent about workers' rights, civil rights, and so forth.

In the 1996 election, Bill Clinton went for the women's vote, so to speak. He said he would keep abortion legal and continued to stand by a woman's right to choose in limited fashion. Hillary silently concurred. In this surreal arena of election politics the two parties seemed to be gender-swapping. The Republican convention appeared feminized with Lizzie Dole working the crowds and Susan Molinari with baby in hand. Those watching were not supposed to pay any attention to the fact that Molinari's vote matched ultra-rightist Newt Gingrich's over 90 percent of the time. Columnist Maureen Dowd called the 1996 convention an "estrogen festival to woo women".4 Meanwhile, the Democrats acted tough, like the stern father, vowing to clean up welfare.

Soon after, the American public was led from one scandal to another with no effect. Bill Clinton was charged with sexual harassment and his friends in the Whitewater affair were found guilty. Hillary found long-lost papers relating to Whitewater on a table in her private quarters and says she does not know where they could have been—and Bill continued to govern. As first-world nations privatize, they call upon the myths of family solidarity of yesteryear. As third-world countries supply girls and women for the global factories, they unsettle traditional patriarchal familial parameters. As a result, sexual and gender politics along with their racial meanings continually change.

Monica Lewinsky, as well as Paula Jones, Gennifer Flowers and Kathleen Willey were alleged to have had sexual encounters of one sort or another with Bill Clinton. Lewinsky, the White House intern who allegedly had oral sex with Bill, created the scandal of a lifetime that followed suit with the impeachment proceedings of 1998 and 1999. Bill said there had been no sex, and Hillary once again stood by her man.

While Monicagate proceeded in 1998 so did the continuation of sanctions on and renewed bombing of Iraq. The newest sex scandal allowed the right wing a perfect diversion. Sex was used to unravel Bill. His lies emboldened the right-wing war agenda.

The continuing war in Iraq began in 1991 and continued in different forms through both the Clinton and Bush administrations. By 1998, when bombing resumed once again, half of Iraqis were already suffering malnutrition; their cancer rates had risen fivefold. The war then was already costing $100,000,000 a day, $2 billion for twenty days.

Madeleine Albright, the first female US Secretary of State, oversaw these early Iraq policies. When she was asked whether she could live with the fact that the sanctions against Saddam Hussein were causing the death of over 500,000 children, she responded that she was willing to pay the price. (This number of deaths is more than those who died in Hiroshima and Nagasaki.) Neither Bill nor Hillary objected. They were hawks on this war. Iraqi families were already eating in rotation then, and their babies were fed sugared water because milk was not available. Yet Hillary never spoke on behalf of these women and children.

Remember these shifting gendered identities as part of Hillary's legacy.

Notes

1   Some of the discussion found here first appeared in my books *Hatreds* (New York: Routledge, 1996); *Global Obscenities* (New York: New York University Press, 1998); *Against Empire* (London: Zed Books, 2004); and *Sexual Decoys* (London: Zed Books, 2007).

2   Beverly Allen, *Rape Warfare: The Hidden Genocide in Bosnia-Herzegovina and Croatia* (Minneapolis: University of Minnesota Press, 1996), p. xii.

3   Raymond Hernandez and Robert Pear, "Once an Enemy, Health Industry Warms to Clinton", *New York Times*, July 12, 2006, p. A1.

4   Maureen Dowd, "Plowshares into Pacifiers", *New York Times*, August 16, 1996, p. A27.

12

Yesterday's Hillary

When Bill and Hillary moved into the White House in 1992 there was much noise about a new kind of Democrat and a new kind of presidential wife. But like much else this promise of a new kind of Democrat only came to partial fruition and not in the way that most people had expected. The new "neoliberal" Democrats looked more like the Republicans as they privatized the government, gutted social welfare, and oversaw, even if they did not initiate, the curtailment of abortion rights. And Hillary was a new kind of First Lady, but not exactly in the way she had promised.

On the one hand Hillary stood for the mass-marketed version of feminism: she is a trained lawyer, well educated and smart, she has a child, she appears aloof and focused on power, she sometimes cares about her maiden name. So even though Hillary, at this time, had never identified herself as a feminist activist, feminism was attached to her. Defame one and hurt the other. It was so much trickier than with Nancy Reagan or Barbara Bush. They stood clearly as wives, not as professionals. They deferred to their husbands in ways that made clear that their first duty was as wife and mother.

They were First Lady to the old kind of nation. Nancy and Barbara did not ask the public to renegotiate their selfhood, and Hillary did. Hillary wanted to rewrite her role as citizen-wife for so-called post-Cold War times. As an active player-coequal-partner she needed new rules; just as global capital needed new rules. But gender changes are even more unsettling than global ones. So her media experts nervously wrote old stories on her: headbands, pageboy hairdos, pink angora sweaters.

Supposedly the First Lady, as a successful professional woman, was one of "us", whoever the "us" was meant to be. The borders of feminism are left fluid and manipulated for the nation: popular culture vaporizes feminism while it privatizes it for the market and depoliticizes it for the state. Hillary was the public conduit for all this negotiation whether she chose to be or not.

Much was at stake in defining the boundary lines of gender— womanhood, manhood, and family life—for the transnational globe. Gender borders are always being reconstructed, and Bill and Hillary were a reminder of this process. Richard Nixon warned of this when he snarled that a strong woman makes a man look weak. This weakness in the national imagination reads as effeminate, or homosexual. No wonder all the upset surrounding Bill's draft dodging, his early foray into the arena of gays in the military, and the subsequent contestation about gay marriage.

It is significant that few politicians in the US at that time identified themselves as feminist although fewer still would have publicly challenged mainstream equal-rights feminism. This absorption and silencing of feminism mainstreamed it to the point that liberal feminism was neutralized as though women were already equal and feminism was no longer needed.

This mix of marketing, mainstreaming, and popularizing *but* also denigrating and silencing feminism blurs the lines between using women as icons for the market and encoding feminist claims. These conflicting processes operate to create the fantasmatic of success: of a Jacqueline Kennedy, a Hillary Clinton, or an Oprah. The mass marketing absorbs, publicizes, normalizes, depoliticizes and disciplines *all at the same time*. The marketing redefines the boundaries between privacy and publicness, inside and outside, mainstream politics and mass culture, feminist language and women's identities. Hillary represented this complex fluidity and became the perfect fictive symbol. Few knew who she was, and few knew who she is.

During Bill's incumbency, Hillary said little about most feminist issues: child-care, prenatal care for poor women, the Equal Rights

Amendment, equal pay, etcetera. Soon after the 1992 election Bill got angry with feminist groups for demanding too many appointments from his administration and called them "bean counters". Hillary said nothing. Then he consecutively nominated Zoe Baird and Kimba Wood for attorney general. Both were successful lawyers who were pressured/forced to step aside because of their nanny problems. Their nannies were undocumented immigrants. Illegal, undocumented workers both stood in for and covered over the problems with child care for professional parents.

The class privilege of Baird and Wood was easy to demonize, positioned as it was against their practices of motherhood; and feminism got encoded through rich white women who hire undocumented workers on the cheap. Every man and woman who has worried about child care felt uncomfortable with the story as it unfolded. Hillary, a lawyer and mom herself, said nothing. It should be remembered that Clinton had to find an unmarried woman with no children, Janet Reno, to fill the attorney general position. She then told us, in code, that she is not a lesbian, and that she really likes men.

The sexual/gender relations of family and nation and globe were changing incoherently, *and* they remain strikingly unchanged. More women enter government, and they still must find day care. There is a family leave act, and women still can't afford to take leave without pay. Hillary chose not to address the punishing gendered chaos.

The initial nomination and then the quick withdrawal of Lani Guinier, a noted African American law professor, for assistant attorney general for civil rights in 1993 revealed the intense political conflict over racial and gender borders for the nation at that time as well. Bill Clinton's "waffling" was not simply a psychological disorder. Waffling is in part a political stance amid unsettling flux, and change.

Guinier's nomination highlights the racial and gender challenges for defining the shifting borders of public spaces. Guinier is a woman of color who was supposed to enforce civil rights for a government that got scared because conservatives called her a "quota queen". Guinier's positions on affirmative action were depicted as too radical. Neither Bill nor Hillary defended her stellar writing and record on race discrimination. Although a friend of Hillary's from before, she was left quickly in the dust.

It is not unimportant that as First Lady Hillary Rodham Clinton was supposed to symbolize the nation at its best. But there was no one narrative that the nation or her gender could easily follow. No one metaphor worked well, so Hillary kept rewriting herself. As such, she embodied rather than resolved the crisis of the nation. Instead of representing a fantasmatic unity she destabilized the boundaries necessary to it. As First Lady she seemed to be too independent and too comfortable with power. And yet she was also simply Bill's wife. This was not the kind of family icon a shaky nation needed then.

During their first term in office Hillary appeared to be courting both her husband and the American public at the same time. She had accepted her glass ceiling, and she would live with it no matter what the cost. She tried to be more involved and knowledgeable and professional than former First Ladies. She got nailed at every turn. People kept asking, "Who elected her, anyway?" while they forgot to ask about all the men in charge we haven't chosen either.

Things became messier yet. Hillary became a scapegoat for men and women who fear feminism. She wasn't a homemaker and soon became the "cookie monster" as she first snubbed her nose at cookie making and then agreed to a cookie bake-off.[1] She unsettled sex/gender borders because she simultaneously represented traditional gender roles and their revision. She provoked hostility because she was First Lady, but not just that. She creates fear and hate because she is both stereotypical of feminism and not enough of a feminist. The tension here was much bigger than Hillary herself.

So she remains polarizing to this day. Supposedly people either hate her or love her. Those who choose to hate her may do so because she reminds them of what they fear in themselves. She stays with a man who has told us all, in so many words, that he "betrayed" her, and he uses her skills to protect himself.

Bill's marital infidelities humanized Hillary as the suffering wife even if they democratized her too much for everyone's liking. Her so-called power feminism was easier to swallow when it looked like victim feminism. The aggressive bitch and castrator was refeminized while Bill the war wimp was remasculinized.

Powerful women often receive little support in the US. Feminism also receives little support from powerful people. Feminism is not necessarily about powerful women, and powerful women are very often not feminist.[2] Hillary, as a mass-marketed icon of feminism, means that women lose if she loses, and most often do not gain when she gains. She continued to accommodate power rather than use it on behalf of women. When Hillary presented the outlines of the healthcare package on Capitol Hill in 1993, she did so positioned *vis-à-vis* a male patriarch: as a wife, a mother, and a daughter. She said she was "proud to serve her country". In this instance Hillary sub-textually advocated a "power feminism" from her position as a devoted citizen with market appeal. According to Tamar Lewin of the *New York Times*, she focused on what women can do, not on what they are kept from doing. She showed "no rage at men, no rhetoric about oppression or empowerment, not even a whisper of a Ms".[3]

Several months later she looked different and talked differently again. The health plan had failed, and Hillary the professional was disciplined: she was domesticated back to her family, once again as simply a wife. By March 1995, she had started to stress women and children's issues as she traveled abroad. It is interesting to see how her focus shifted when she left the US. Once outside its borders she spoke readily on behalf of poor women in India. In New Delhi, she found a new voice in which to read a young girl's poem titled "Silence". The clearly feminist poem asks for an end to women's silences.[4]

While in India Hillary met with the Self-Employed Women's Association which assists women in the largely invisible and informal economy of self-employed women.[5] She was very taken with their organization and praised its results in addressing women's poverty. From this space outside the US, Hillary criticized the "rampant materialism and consumerism" of Western countries.[6] She reinscribed the East–West divide in her depiction of women's lives in South Asia. She stated: "When I think about the women who've been imprisoned, tortured, discouraged, barred from involvement in education or professional opportunity — what any of us in America go through is minor in comparison."[7] Though Hillary meant to highlight and condemn the official, state-mandated torture of women in other countries, she inadvertently slighted the gross inequities affecting many women in the West. She legitimated, even if unintentionally, the quieting of feminist voices at home.

Hillary has a history of speaking as a feminist when she is outside US borders: when she visited other countries, and at United Nations conferences on women. She took feminism, as an export, abroad. She defined the "backwardness" of India as the backdrop for her concerns with "girls and women", which became a "human rights" issue.[8] Strangely enough, because she was speaking about children some in the media then called her a traditional First Lady. Wrong again.

Just as transnational capital appeared triumphant across the globe, women gathered in Beijing in 1995 to say their needs were not being met. This moment in Beijing starkly contrasts with the privatized and individualist global discourses of that day. Women gathered and said, for the world to hear, that governments throughout the five continents must commit to ending sex discrimination and act affirmatively on behalf of women's rights.

Hillary spoke at Beijing. And then she spoke again, in Belfast in 1997. She spoke about how women can improve their nations, saying that "when women are empowered to make the most of their own potential then their families will thrive. And when families thrive, communities and nations thrive as well."⁹ But what did this actually, tangibly, mean for women in this time of the dominance of transnational capital? And I am hesitant to accept Hillary's choice to reinscribe women in their families, for their nations.

She used the development approach that encodes women's labor as that of mothers responsible for their families. This particular development discourse reproduces aspects of patriarchy and women's secondary status while modernizing the forms in which they occur. Using it, Hillary re-encodes this sexual and gender politics for first- and third-world countries alike.

Hillary was called just about everything when First Lady because neither she nor the nation knew what she needed to be.¹⁰ She merely embodied the changing familial structures of the nation during globalization of the market while the nation needed more fluid borders than the racial/gender structure could easily deliver.

Bill and Hillary, as a presidential couple, were defined by each other. Hillary was too domineering; Bill waffled. Bill runs and has thunder thighs and loves junk food; Hillary likes vegetables. Bill talks too much and too long and is too empathetic. Hillary is short and curt. Bill is a womanizer, a survivor of an alcoholic and abusive father. Hillary knew how to cope with all this.

The feminizing of Bill and masculinizing of Hillary point to the complex processes that continue to redefine gender and with it the US. Bill and Hillary were our postmodern therapeutic couple. They know how to survive. They were, and are, willing to change, again, and again.

So after the humiliation of the Lewinsky scandal Hillary decided to run for the Senate seat in New York, and to reclaim herself. The First Lady decided to be the first First Lady to run for senator of New York. It wasn't clear in 2000 that she could put all the scandal and noise behind her and win, but she did.

Bill and Hillary at present have a home together in Chappaqua, New York, although he lives there most of the time by himself. She has a home in Washington DC as well. As

Senator, and before the 2008 presidential primaries, Hillary continued to defend her early vote to support the war in Iraq. She defended her repeated authorizations to re-fund the war as well. It appeared that she valued being seen as aggressive and decisive about the war above all else. She thought John Murtha's call for immediate withdrawal was "a big mistake".

As time went on and there was more and more criticism of the war, Hillary finally queried its inadequate strategies, but without questioning the wisdom for going to war. Finally, she publicly dressed down Donald Rumsfeld for botching the war and she said that too many strategic blunders created a failed situation of mismanagement. Eventually, she joined others in Congress calling for an exit strategy, but with no set withdrawal date.

Hillary's voice is more often than not militarist. She defended Israel in what she termed its 2006 defensive bombings towards Hezbollah in Lebanon, and said the US will stand behind Israel because Israel stands for American values. She voted against Senator Diane Feinstein's resolution to forbid the use of cluster bombs in Iraq, even though cluster bombs disproportionately maim civilians, especially children.

During her first term as Senator, Hillary along with the Feminist Majority hosted a Forum on the Future of Women in Afghanistan on the importance of women in the reconstruction of their country. At the hearings, many of the Afghan women present spoke about the importance of support from US women's groups and yet raised their fear of a cultural imperialism that does not fully understand Afghan women's particular situations.

Hillary was not particularly attuned to this concern. She, like the Feminist Majority, a US liberal feminist activist group which was crucial in first bringing the plight of Afghan women to the attention of the world, did not criticize US policies for past support of the Taliban during Afghanistan's war against the Soviet Union. They both ignored women activists in Afghanistan and in exile as well as the wide swath of feminisms that exist within the Muslim world. Most Muslim feminists argue that the

US must rethink its foreign policy as a whole, particularly in the Middle East. Hillary Clinton's strategies have ignored these complex relations between imperial politics, militarism, and women's rights.

The 1992 and 1996 Clinton administrations ended more than a decade ago. And yet they are also very present. Hillary remains a conduit for the fluidity of changing gender, as well as someone stuck in yesterday. She no longer is the new woman on the block. And she still remains Bill's wife. Her hair is more closely cropped and does not change much anymore. She is always wearing pantsuits. She genders herself carefully but not bravely, nor newly enough.

Remember all this messy history, too.

Notes

1   Karen Lehrman, "Beware the Cookie Monster," *New York Times*, July 18, 1992, p. A23.

2   Gary Wills, "H. R. Clinton's Case", *New York Review of Books*, vol. XXXIX, no. 5 (March, 1992), pp. 3–5.

3   Tamar Lewin, "A Feminism that Speaks For Itself", *New York Times*, October 3, 1993, p. 2E.

4   Todd Purdum, "Hillary Clinton's Trip: Women's Voice", *New York Times*, March 30, 1995, p. A6.

5   (AP), "Hillary Clinton Talks to Poor Working Women's Group in India", *New York Times*, March 31, 1995, p. A7.

6   Todd Purdum, "First Lady Holds Forth, Long Distance", *New York Times*, March 20, 1995, p. A13.

7   As quoted in "Hillary Clinton Talks to Poor Working Women's Group in India".

8   Todd Purdum, "Hillary Clinton, A Traditional First Lady Now", *New York Times*, April 6, 1995, p. A1.

9   Quoted in Sarah Lyall, "Hillary Clinton Sees Hope in Ulster, Too", *New York Times*, November 1, 1997, p. A6.

10 Michael Kelly, "Saint Hillary", *New York Times* Magazine, May 23, 1993, pp. 22–66.

13

A Post-New Hampshire Diary of Sorts

I have already said that race and gender morph and change and evolve. It should therefore be no surprise that they continued to do so through the 2008 presidential primary season. I write of this process here as I observed it unfolding at the time.

There are horrible and painful racial, gender, sex and class divides in the US. The fact that Barack and Hillary both ran for president does little to change this reality. Yet even at the start of the campaign, it was evident to everyone that their candidacies represented enormous change from the times that black slavery existed or no woman—white and black—or black man had the right to vote, or to get an education. Despite these changes, not enough has changed, and what has changed is often mis-represented and misunderstood. Needless to say, Obama and Clinton, in their campaigns, often invoked an equality that does not yet fully exist. But this commitment to equality remains useful as a promissory for change and hope.

When pundits and journalists spoke and wrote about the racial and gendered reality at the start of the campaign I thought they were somewhat off in this description. It was because neither Barack nor Hillary bespoke the existing norm, the stan-dardized white man, that race and gender were named. After all, race and gender were present when in the past white men ran against each other for president. But whiteness and maleness were left as the silenced standard in all the previous instances. Their silent privilege bespeaks their specific status as a universal, non-particular one.

In the 2008 primary season, Barack's race and Hillary's gender deviated from the established standard; for this reason, gender and race were named as issues, and divisive ones at that.

However, much of the language surrounding this discussion has been less than helpful and distorts the complexities at hand. Barack is black (actually mixed-race) *and* a male; and Hillary is not just female, she is *also* white. Simply naming Barack as black normalizes the fact that he is a man; and identifying Hillary as a woman naturalizes her whiteness. Yet, each of them represents a race *and* a gender, if not plural races and genders, so a simple dichotomizing of them is unhelpfully polarizing.

Besides, our language's phrasing about "blacks and women" falsely ignores the complex reality that there are black women. When race is said to be the new divide in Iowa, or New Hampshire, or South Carolina—that Barack will get the black vote, and Hillary the white vote—I am left to wonder, are the whites here mainly white women? And/or white men? And where do black women line up in this solipsistic phrasing?

Much has changed and continues to change in terms of race and gender, and how race is gendered, and gender is raced, and much also has not changed. Election rhetoric reaffirms what has not changed when it describes women as though they are all white, or blacks as though they are all men. Yet Barack at the start made clear he was not running as black, and Hillary made clear she was not standing as a woman. This identification also shifts. There were a myriad of race and gender stories to unfold by the time we got to the end.

Hillary morphed from not being a woman and rather a person of experience, into a tough commander-in-chief, into someone who needed to "find her own voice", with a softer, kinder, more humanized cadence. Barack tried to stay away from simply being black, but morphed to delivering a speech on race, to mobilizing black and Latina women voters.

The world is now economically defined and structured by a newly complex global capitalist market where people of color are a more visible majority, and whites are a minority. It is no surprise then that it might be time for a black president, much like the time came when the slave plantation system was no longer needed for a more industrial America.

Abolitionism was often a movement for racial equality, but often it was not. It would be wrong to assume that the racial divides will melt away this time. Although women are newly elected as heads of state more often than in the past, global transnational corporations have the upper hand against the nation state today. So, women as leaders in formerly-more-powerful nation states may not simply be what they seem.

Power itself shifts and changes with and alongside the meanings of race and gender. It is fascinating that the changes in race and gender are always connected and still often not parallel. Hence, Obama made it clear throughout his campaign that he did not want anyone to vote for him because he is black, and Hillary in contrary and even in complex fashion finally asked women to vote for her because she would break the glass ceiling for them.

Maybe Barack's deep appeal was that he promised something beyond race and gender. He almost seemed androgynous: neither macho nor feminine but something new and fluid. His ambiguous color and body type could not be easily stereotyped. On the other hand, Hillary in her gender-armored pantsuits seemed stuck in her past "experience".

Hillary tried too hard at first to *not* be female in the hopes that she might be taken seriously. She then tried too hard to be simply female. The misogyny directed at Hillary was outrageous at the start: the criticism of her showing her cleavage, and of her cackle-type laugh, the calling her a "bitch". The rub here is that Hillary sidestepped confrontation with misogyny at this point in time. But she also continued to make mistakes at every turn.

She encouraged the racial and gender divide in the hopes that would get her the white male and female vote. She did this at any cost. When all else failed, she ran as Bill's wife, again not as a courageous and independent anti-racist woman. As "Bill's wife", she could not speak honestly and forthrightly about how the discriminatory treatment towards her reflected that we all still live in a white man's world that needs fundamental change.

It is also a bit of a mystery that Hillary could not seem like more of an agent for/of change than she did. She instead was caught remaking the old—Bill's old-boy political networks, and worn-out Iraq policies. And she never seemed to notice that in comparison to wives like Michelle Obama and Elizabeth Edwards, rather than Laura Bush, she needed an update. In 1992 Hillary promised herself as a co-president that was newly different at the time. But when she promised Bill in 2008 as her newest rendition of her co-presidency it did not translate.

The footing had shifted for Hillary, but she did not get it. Even if not enough had changed in the previous decade, too much had changed to make her run for president remarkable in and of itself. Gender has become too complex for such a simplistic politics. Barack did start to get it and the interplay of race and gender shifted for him. He challenged Hillary on her manipulations and her purported claim on women. He articulated a progressive agenda that recognized the difficulties of single parents like his mother and committed to making changes that would embolden women of all kinds.

Neither presidential candidate was up to speed on feminisms of the present day. There are as many kinds of feminism(s) as there are ideas about what a woman is, can be, or should be. In part this is because one's sex, as in female, does not automatically clarify one's notion of gender, as in one's notion of womanhood. Or, as Simone de Beauvoir stated years ago: one is born female and becomes a woman.[1] The woman we choose to be is complex, and plural, and not homogeneous.

The primary season continued and Hillary remained unclear about who she is. Early on she said gender was not an issue. She said it was her experience, especially as First Lady, that qualified her for the job. As such, she is not her own person; she is Bill's wife, again. As months of the primary season passed, Hillary dropped the Rodham, and promised black voters—mainly women voters in South Carolina—that if they voted for her it would be like the Bill Clinton years again.

But contradictions continued to abound. She said that any individual can be president and then also offered that she is glad to be the first female to run for president. She denied that her opponents criticized her because she is a woman, saying they did it simply because she was winning in the polls at the time, and then she went to Wellesley, the all-women college she graduated from, especially to mobilize young female voters. She spoke about how she likes the "heat of the kitchen" and therefore can win. And then, making a claim about gender change, she quoted the popular phrase "sometimes the best man for the job is a woman", while promising to win in the "all-boys club of presidential politics". Hillary repeatedly brought up the woman thing, and then closed it down, until the very end of the campaign, when she had nothing left to lose.

Barack gained against Hillary as he exposed her self-proclaimed experience as too much a part of "politics as usual". She had mobilized the formidable Clinton machine, but took her usual second place to Bill by doing so. No male presidential candidate had the problematic "wife" status to deal with like Hillary. But she could not address this particular status because she is so bound and gagged by it.

Hillary remained caught between a rock—being a woman—and a hard place—not being a woman—as the presidential debates unfolded. She refused to answer the question of whether she would appoint only pro-abortion judges if president. Instead she used a coded language supportive of the right to privacy. Women's bodies and their rights to reproductive choice were never mentioned. Barack followed suit with evasion as well.

Sometimes, Hillary revealed more than she might wish. She voted with the arch-conservative Rick Santorum and co-sponsored the Workplace Religious Freedom Act which allows workers to refuse to perform key aspects of their jobs on the basis of their religious beliefs. Pharmacists could refuse to fill birth control prescriptions or police officers could refuse to guard abortion clinics. Really, Hillary?

Hillary remained a cautious follower on Iraq despite Barack's more popular anti-war stance. Midway through the primaries she still did not support Barbara Lee's bill to prevent permanent military bases in Iraq and deny further funding for anything other than costs related to the safe deployment of US troops home. Instead, Hillary continued to play it safe as a tough commander-in-chief. Then came her advertising blitz that asked everyone who they would want answering the phone in the middle of the night in the White House if there were an emergency.

Hillary did not want to risk being identified as a feminist, or too feminine, or too soft, or too whatever. Instead, she endorsed too much of the old gendered masculinist rhetoric. She did not get that the country was too tired of Bush's and Cheney's tough guy stance. Given all this, she said too little that was new, and did too little to mobilize women until too late.

It is unfair that gender—even in its changed and modernized form—continues to matter in unfair and unjust ways. So Hillary could not make gender irrelevant because it counts too much in the way that political culture is structured. She pretended she was running on her own individual record and tried to cleanse herself of feminist rhetoric and symbolism, and yet she couldn't do this successfully because gender politics is bigger than any one individual. Her neoliberal individualism, embedded as it is in misogyny, could not help her out here.

Hillary was similar and different to her male opponents, much like gender itself. Gender is never simply an either/or option. A November 2007 CBS poll found that Hillary was thought to be the best person for overseeing a war as commander-in-chief; Barack was found to be more likeable and more likely to create change. At this point in the primaries, people thought Hillary could win the presidency, and said they might vote for her because of this, but would choose to spend an evening with Barack, rather than her, if given the choice.

Although Hillary sometimes regendered herself in order not to be incorrectly gendered as a soft female, the public regendered her yet again by viewing her within the old man/woman divide. In all this fluid mix Obama as a black man interestingly, and maybe unexpectedly, became the non-threatening male and Hillary as the white woman became the militarized, unlikeable female. Men become the new women—and women, the new men—with unexpected variations and twists and turns.

A key moment came in March 2007, in Selma, Alabama. Both Hillary and Barack wanted to lay claim to its important role in the civil rights movement. Barack said he was black enough to know that his roots are in Selma; Hillary said that she celebrated the struggles that started here. They each were courting the black vote; he as a black man that some said was not black enough, she as a (white) woman who is married to Bill who had once been referred to as the US's first black president.

Whenever there is gender switching or flux, there is also racial morphing. Hillary ran, in some sense, as a white man—experienced and tough—and Barack was depicted by Hillary as inexperienced, and by default like a black woman. Yet Hillary still courted the black woman's vote. Hillary meanwhile promised black women that if they voted for her she would deliver Bill. Supposedly, early on, black women favored Bill over Barack.

Black women are neither simply black nor female, but simultaneously both black and female. Obama is neither simply black nor a (white) man. Hillary is both white and a woman. Hillary and Barack are both gendered and raced. He should not silence gender because Hillary is female; nor silence race because he fears being re-gendered black.

Many black women identify with both aspects of their racial and gendered selves. They are black women and felt aligned with Barack because he is black, and with Hillary because she is female. Hillary, with little regard for this double consciousness, asked black women to break barriers with her. She asked them to identify with her as female. She asked them if a (white) woman can be president and answered, "yes". "The great thing about America" is that anyone can be President. It "just depends on the individual". In asking them to be female, she asked them not to be black. Inadvertently, at best, she asked them to be white.

Obama gave his speech to the nation on race in order to deflect and redirect all the noise about Reverend Wright. Barack had been made blacker as the campaign continued, and Hillary next shifted her focus to the "hard-working working class", silently read as white.

Gender and with it race were deployed and contradictorily redeployed over and over again.

Note

1   Simone de Beauvoir, *The Second Sex* (New York: Penguin, 1972).

14

The Audaciousness of Race

First, let me make a mention of a bit of my own race story, given that I am white and writing this. I grew up in the civil rights era. I moved with my family to Atlanta, Georgia, in 1964 where my father would teach at Atlanta University's predominantly black graduate center. It was a time of racial integration. We lived in the black neighborhood on Beckwith Street and I went to the newly desegregated white school that had just admitted its first black student that year. Shortly after moving there, I would walk through my black neighborhood and be called a "white bitch". By the time I reached school after passing through the surrounding poor white neighborhood I was a "nigger lover".

My mother came to know a much-respected black surgeon in Atlanta through civil rights demonstrations, often held in front of Lester Maddox's Pickrick restaurant. When she was diagnosed with breast cancer that year she asked Dr Asa Yancey to be her surgeon. But at that time he did not have hospital privileges other than at the black hospital. So my mother had her surgery performed in the black hospital. Years later when I read her FBI file I saw that my mother was identified as black. It took me a minute to realize the mistaken assumption: that a black hospital meant a black woman. Who says race is not fluid and constructed? And yet race also remains complexly differentiated for people with black and brown and yellow skin.

Given the rancorous racialized and gendered hyperbole of the 2008 presidential Democratic primary election, it became more important than usual to rethink and revisit the way racial privilege is relationally constructed. Obama was repeatedly asked to address his "race problem"—even before the Reverend Wright controversy—while early on Hillary was given a pass on her gender. Hillary Clinton never was asked or expected to address the "problem" of gender *per se*.

One might respond that Obama had to address the racial fall-out after the YouTubing of his pastor Jeremiah Wright's angry anti-white rhetoric. But this does not explain the central place of race in the campaign despite Barack's wishes otherwise. Gender was never similarly posed as a problem for Hillary to negotiate, even if the misogyny of the election process defined her parameters. Hillary was never raced or gendered like Obama. He was often raced against his wishes, while Hillary was once again e-raced as having a race. She was silently white, while Obama was made noisily black. And she embraced her gendering "as a woman" strategically and politically even if inconsistently, while he chose to not speak as black, or for blacks.

Whereas Hillary proclaimed that her candidacy was important because it would break the glass ceiling of gender, during the primaries Barack never claimed race as part of his political capital. However, a strategy of the Clinton campaign was to make Barack's race a deficit for him. It was Hillary's strategy in order to triumph. If Obama were made black enough, Hillary could win because she is white. She would win because she is white, and not black, and not because she is a woman speaking on behalf of women's rights.

As long as she sought support from Reagan Democrats—white male working- and middle-class voters—she veered away from a woman-centered gender politics. Even though the strategizing reduced the question of race to the privilege of whiteness it also craftily subsumed the presence of gender to an invisible status. With race always having a gender, and gender always being defined through one's race, this reduction of race to its own singular self distorts the doubled both-ness of Barack and Hillary. Gender is subsumed inside race; and race becomes white.

My point is that the contest between Hillary and Barack was never simply or only about or between races; nor about gender in opposition to race. The terms "race" and racism are mystifying of "whiteness" in and of themselves. Racism in the US usually bespeaks white privilege even though there are racisms within communities of color(s). In the case of Hillary, her white privilege sometimes trumps her gender identity. Being white posed no problem for Hillary like being black posed for Barack as he struggled to be seen for who he thinks he is.

Geraldine Ferraro's comment that if Barack Obama were white he wouldn't be running for president, became quite well known during the primaries. She added that he also would not be running—with his limited credentials—if he were a woman. She believed that his race benefited him unfairly; that being black was an asset for him. I must say that even my most reticent and conservative students couldn't fathom this statement.

I guess Ferraro was ignoring or forgetting about blacks in the prisons, their poverty index, and their unemployment and underemployment rates. She assumed Barack was falsely worthy, and had stolen Hillary's rightful chance at victory. This racialized rancor sounds too similar to the affirmative action Bakke legal case: a white law student claimed that an unqualified black had stolen his expected place in law school.

According to Ferraro's logic, if Hillary were black she would have been better situated to handily win the nomination. But if Hillary were black she probably would not be married to Bill Clinton who happens to be white. And if she weren't married to Bill she would not have had the necessary experience she claimed to have. Also, it is unlikely, at least up to this point in political history, that Hillary would be a key political player if she were part of an interracial marriage. Maybe being black is not all that Ferraro and the Hillary campaign claimed that it was.

Hillary counted on the white and Latina vote—be it older female voters or working-class men—to win the primaries. She worked hard to pull these voters towards herself and away from Barack. As time passed and Hillary was losing the delegate votes that she needed, she became more gender conscious in response to white female voters, who had become her most devoted constituency. These women activated Hillary more than she mobilized them. She had finally become a (white) feminist even if a bit against her will.

It has always been problematic for me that US feminism is most often assumed to be a white women's thing despite the fact that so many of the earliest campaigns, against sexual harassment and for workers' rights, were first articulated and fought by black women. In South Carolina Obama won 54 percent of the women's vote with 22 percent of white women voting for him; 78 percent of black women did. It should also be recognized that black women overwhelmingly—well more than 90 percent—voted Democrat in the last Bush/Cheney presidential election. Many more white women than black voted for Bush.

Nothing I have written so far is uncomplicatedly true. Quickly to surmise: the relations between race and gender are growing more complex and porous and fluid. Yet static oppositions between them continue to prevail. Obama's gender is racialized, and his race is gendered. This is similar for Hillary. It is not gender versus race. And it is not black versus white. Obama was suckled and mothered by a white woman. His maternal grandparents are white. His Kenyan father was black African. He is made of both these genetic and cultural histories.

The Reverend Wright controversy became an excuse to mobilize the dormant racialized aspects of this primary season. Obama chose finally to come at "race" *per se* head-on. Initially, he said he deplored the divisiveness of some of Wright's statements, and yet Wright was family, like his white grandmother who also sometimes expressed unkind racial views. His family bespeaks the contradictions of the larger society—prejudices and love existing side by side, at the same time. He knows first-hand that these tensions and contradictions are workable. Yet, he also makes a painful break with Reverend Wright. He tells us that there is a more hopeful racial story today than before. He thinks there is a good possibility for meaningful change. That the US can move through and beyond its present racial conflicts. He asks us all to move on from here.

Hillary kept the Wright controversy alive because this allowed her whiteness to remain a silent weapon. She said, when asked what she thought of Reverend Wright, "he would not be my pastor". In this moment Hillary chose her whiteness and her gender to position herself against Wright, and his and Barack's black identity.

At this point in the campaigning, Obama was winning one primary after the next. Hillary had lost serious ground and seemed destined for defeat. Bill Richardson, governor of New Mexico and former high-ranking member of Bill Clinton's administration, finally endorsed Obama. He did this saying it was time for the party to recognize that Obama was the chosen candidate—by the number of states won, by chosen delegates, and by popular vote—and move on to form a viable candidacy for the fall election. Many observers and pundits said that it was all but impossible for Clinton to win the nomination at this point. Several even said that if it were Barack that had Hillary's delegate numbers and popular vote, the race would have already been called.

By this time there was a groundswell. Almost everyone said that unless Hillary had a blowout in Pennsylvania and the remaining primaries, and then got the support of super delegates, she was done. But why did she keep going? And why was there such disbelief that she had lost? And what did they mean by a blowout? They meant and thought that she still might get the white vote in all its many variations: Latinas, Catholics, the working class, Reagan democrats, older women, and so on.

But Hillary did not do it. She did not win the primaries. The primaries became a post-racial, though not a post-racist moment. And so I was pleased, but also wondered what Barack had just won and what would happen next.

I was not feeling conflicted or wondering about Hillary's loss. I was with my sister Julia, who said that the only woman she wanted to see in the White House after this whole long slugfest was Michelle.

15

Hillary Is White

It was already late into the bruising Democratic primary struggle. I wrote this piece in order to criticize, as an anti-racist feminist, what I thought was an emerging troubled relationship between racism and feminism in the presidential campaign. This writing was posted on www.CommonDreams.org and made its way into multiple language translations across the globe. Men and women of color from all over the world, especially Africans and African Americans in the US, contacted me with their generous affirmation of its message.

In May 2008 it already seemed pretty certain that Barack Obama would be the Democratic nominee in the fall. Even though this was the case, and maybe because this was so evident to many of us, it seemed more crucial than ever to clarify how wrong-headed Hillary Clinton's campaign had been. Otherwise, feminists of all sorts would be left with the bad taste of feminist racism to deal with, once again. I was looking ahead to help build the possibility of a newly invigorated multi-racial, multi-class-based feminism/ womanism both here and abroad.

At this post-Indiana, post-North Carolina, post-West Virginia presidential primary moment, few TV pundits and newspaper journalists appeared to wonder or worry about the particular exclusion of black women from election discourse. Instead, most eyes, and especially Hillary's and Bill's, were focused on the so-called (white) "hard-working working class". Hillary's pre-occupation with white voters was a dead give-away of how she thinks about gender, and about being a woman. Gender is white to her, like race is black. Bill and Hillary Clinton threw African Americans to the wind as a last-ditch strategy for victory. They thought they could play the gender card with its history of whiteness and win.

And here lies the rub. As election rhetoric evolved, Hillary Clinton became "the" woman who wanted to break the glass ceiling of/for gender. But the truth is that at the same time that Hillary became more of a "woman" *per se*, and therefore more of a feminist, she also became more "white". She could ignore her own race, in a way that Obama could not, because of the normalized privileging of whiteness. In this instance white is not a color, but *the* color, *the* standard, by which others are judged.

So Hillary silently, inadvertently but also knowingly, used her color to write her meanings of gender and mobilize older white women and angry white men by doing so. She presented herself as a woman but her real power in this instance was her whiteness. Misogyny—the fear, hatred, punishment, and discrimination toward women—remained a source of harm for Hillary. However, her whiteness coded and continues to code her gender with this privileging of racialized power.

Usually, if a woman is white, the term white is not spoken alongside the term woman; there is thought to be no need. One only specifies color when it is *not* white. And women are assumed to be white if not specified otherwise, especially if you are speaking about gender inequities, or women's rights, or feminism. Forget the reality that black women in the US, first as slaves and then as domestic laborers, factory workers, working mothers, and civil and human rights activists, have long been the trailblazers for women of all colors.

During the presidential primaries Hillary would speak of herself as a woman, and then would speak separately about race, as though she did not embody both at the same time. She has as much "race" as Barack, but her race was not a problem for her like it was for him, even though it may not have been as much of a problem as she tried to make it. Her whiteness privileged and pitted her gender against his race. She encoded her whiteness as central to her gender, and to her kind of feminism, without saying a word.

Hillary reawakened and newly rewrote the history of nineteenth-century US feminism that pitted black men getting the vote against white women's right to the vote. Women's rights rhetoric, since September 11, 2001, has been used in similar fashion to justify the bombing of brown people in Afghanistan and Iraq. Feminism has a history of being bankrupt on this issue of white privilege, so there is little new here. Yet women's rights come, or should come, in all colors.

Obama says he wants to embrace the "newest" notions of race, and with them the racial progress that has occurred. He is not post-racist, but recognizes newly raced relations, as they exist at present. He delivered a much-hailed speech on race although he was not, and does not wish to be, a racial candidate. He recognizes that the country has new-old racial hierarchies with complex new meanings. He embodies these meanings, inasmuch as he is both white and African.

At this same time, Hillary gave no address on or about gender during the campaign. Her campaign officials complained that her unfair media treatment reflected misogyny, but Hillary remained mute on the issues of patriarchy and sexual discrimination while she still hoped to win. Instead of tackling masculinist privilege she became a gun-toting, pro-militarist woman, who curried favor with angry white Reagan Democrats.

Feminisms of all sorts have moved beyond the idea that feminism is a white woman's thing, or that feminisms should be particularly beholden to the white mainstreamed part of the US women's movement, even if some white feminists have not. Large numbers of women, especially women of color, but also anti-racist white women, know that race and gender should be understood as inseparable. This is why most of these women, with their many colors, voted for Barack, whereas Hillary mobilized older white women who saw gender as a homogeneous white formation.

Despite Hillary's wish to crack the glass ceiling of gender, she accepted many of the enforced gender boundaries and kept them in place. She extended the practices of masculinism/misogyny as a female would-be commander-in-chief. She remained female in body and hence could easily parade as a decoy for feminist claims. Her white self was central to this decoy status. She was not simply what she seemed.

Susan Faludi wrote in the *New York Times* that Hillary was having success with white male supporters because she was willing to battle and engage in rough play like one of the boys. She was supposedly willing to "join the brawl" and as such had won their confidence. She had "broke through the glass floor and got down with the boys", opening the way for women to finally make it "through the glass ceiling and into the White House".[1] Barbara Ehrenreich in *The Nation* hesitantly drew from this assessment and then more forcefully criticized Clinton for her ruthlessness. Ehrenreich wrote that Clinton had "smashed the myth of innate female moral superiority in the worst possible way ... demonstrating female moral inferiority".[2]

Hillary has proven that sometimes the best man for the job may be a female posing as a man. In other words, Hillary simply clothed herself in men's tactics and strategies. She can nuke with the best of them. As said in her own words, the US can deliver "the total obliteration" of Iran.

Hillary's embrace of a masculinist machismo authorized the very misogyny that many feminists wish to dismantle. Instead of challenging the gender divide Hillary simply slid over to the other side of it. Instead of offering a new vision of what it might mean to have a female president she offered old versions of masculinist white privilege and warmongering. Nevertheless, many (white) women were unimpressed, like Marie Cocco who wrote in the *Washington Post* (May 15, 2008) that she wouldn't miss the misogyny of the campaign when it was over—she listed the sexist T-shirts and other commercial goods circulating.

Neither Hillary nor any female should be demeaned for being

a woman. But being a woman comes in all colors and economic classes and in sexual variety. Hillary did the unforgivable. She used race—the whiteness card—on behalf of gender. We, the big "we"—the huge diversely defined feminisms in the US and across the globe—are better than this. US black feminists during the 1970s and 1980's women's movement broke open the race/gender divide to show the relationship that exists between them. They exist side by side. Every one of us is both, and more. Only when whiteness parades as an invisible standard can you think that gender and race are separate.

Being female is not enough to allow one to claim one's gender as a political tactic. Such claims must be rooted in a commitment to end gender discrimination with its racial and class formulations; not pit races and classes against each other in the hope of becoming the first woman president. Clinton does not share a political identity with women of all classes and colors and nations simply because she has a female body. She would first need to claim that body and demand rights for it with a multi-racial woman's agenda. She had no multiracial woman's agenda because she had no anti-racist agenda.

Hillary was thrilled when she won big in West Virginia, even though it was already too late in the game for her. She told her followers West Virginia was "almost heaven". She rallied them further when she said that her victory showed that she could win the "hardworking white Americans" in November. But West Virginia is not heaven, nor is it like much of the rest of the country. It is disproportionately white. It is disproportionately old. It may look like what the US used to be, but that is exactly the point.

Let me return to my initial purpose. Given all that had happened during the battle of Hillary and Barack against each other by May 2008, it seemed to me crucial to remember the big "we"—the "we" that spans racial, gender, sexual, and class differences. This meant building a coalition that would make sure that a non-misogynist agenda was part of the anti-racist politics of the rest of the Obama presidential campaign, and then his administration.

Building such an agenda was the new business at hand. Whether Hillary would eventually become a part of this process remained unclear as the primary season neared its end. She still hoped that the same country that had put more than fifty women into space would launch a woman into the White House. But, as I have argued so far, simply being female is not good enough.

True to the way gender continually shifts, Hillary looked a lot more feminist once Sarah Palin became a part of the election scene. And, after all the anger of the primary battle, who would have imagined that Hillary would become Barack's Secretary of State? Yet gender, race, and feminisms continue to evolve.

Notes

1   Susan Faludi, "The Fight Stuff", *New York Times*, May 9, 2008, p. A27.
2   Barbara Ehrenreich, "Hillary's Gift to Women", *The Nation*, May 12, 2008, p. 9.

16

Michelle Is Obviously Black

It is July 2008—it is before Barack won the election. It is before the inaugural and the celebration of Michelle as First Lady. It is important to remember what happened during this "before" period.

Early on in the presidential campaign, Michelle Obama came under special scrutiny for her forthrightness and supposed (racial) anger. The same media that in the end had decried the sexist treatment of Hillary during the primaries were silent as a racialized misogyny went out in force hunting for Michelle. I was bothered that there was so little visible outrage about the racialized misogyny being used to depict and distort Michelle Obama as militant and unpatriotic.

Black feminists asked me where the white feminists were who should be supporting Michelle. Why was there not more of an outcry by Hillary's feminist supporters now that Michelle was caricatured and demonized as someone she is not? It appeared that misogyny is much more readily recognized in its white forms.

Another way of thinking through this query is to wonder whether the US is ready for Michelle as their (black) First Lady. This once again requires an open and bold conversation about race, and particularly about the specific way race is simultaneously defined by and defining of gender. It is significant that the electorate was queried on whether race was a factor in their choice for president, but there was little to no querying about whether they were ready for Michelle as the first black woman to oversee the "white" house. There was so much noise and distortion about who Michelle was with so little analysis of what these depictions meant and reflected.

When it comes to mainstream politics, the lack of querying or discussion about issues of misogyny and male privilege is not new. This silencing underpins the usual relegation of First Lady to a non-issue. But First Lady is hardly an unimportant office, just like the meanings and constructions of gender are neither unimportant or statically given. It matters greatly who the First Lady is and what she does; and when a First Lady steps out of line she is quickly disciplined. When Pat Nixon acted too rich or Hillary Clinton too professional they were readily scrutinized. Interestingly, Barbara and Laura Bush seem to have followed established patriarchal rules carefully enough that they needed little public critique.

Michelle qualifies for being a First Lady given that she is female; but she is also black, and black women have their own history and story to tell here. And these are stories that right-wing conservatives and their bloggers continue either to ignore or to distort. There is no one construction of womanhood or of a First Lady for that matter, and yet all of the latter have been white. Michelle reminds us that gender can have many meanings *and* that gender is also racialized, because she is black. So to be a black female is not one and the same with being a white woman.

The well-publicized cartoon on the cover of the *New Yorker* magazine put Michelle in an Afro while toting a gun. She was made into everyone's supposed worst nightmare: a militant black woman reminiscent of Angela Davis, or maybe the newly militarized women in several African nations. She was made into the ball-busting (black) woman who terrorizes men in general, and white men very particularly.

The New Yorker—call it cartoon, or satire, or whatever—put in clear view the "anti-black (woman) and anti-Muslim as First Lady" scenario that circulated freely in parts of American culture. I can also imagine an alternative cartoon of sorts—with Michelle's coifed hairdo, Jackie O dresses and pearls, her two charming daughters, and Barack holding a bible. This might seem like the left's nightmare fantasy but it is also in stark contrast to the right-wing's lies. This is simply satire in reverse. Lies that are supposed to depict lies end up authorizing them.

At the start of the primaries Michelle was very important to the racialized depiction of Barack because it had been so hard to construct him as an angry black man. Actually, it was easier to depict him as "weak", as too compromising, as too "cool", and even "icy". If Barack was successful with any part of his campaign message, it was that he was not angry—that he believed the US needed a re-visioned model for dealing with racism in its newly complex forms—and that this "newness" unites us more than it divides us.

Given Obama's newly raced image, Michelle became the conduit for racing him as the former kind of angry black. She was depicted as supposedly authentically black: she grew up in Chicago with two black parents in a black neighborhood. Black authenticity was constructed in terms of disaffection and race consciousness in this instance. Michelle was used to make Barack more black.

Michelle was made central to the "othering" of Barack on the cover of the *New Yorker*. Why else put them *both* on the cover? He alone would have been enough given the article inside. But Michelle was necessary. She is the dark-skinned one from the South Side of working-class black Chicago. Barack is mixed-race, lighter-skinned, and grew up in Hawaii—barely stereo-typically authentic.

It was Michelle, and not Barack, who wrote a thesis while at Princeton about one's racial responsibility to one's home community after an elite education. It was Michelle's querying of her own personal obligation to struggles for racial equality that led to the charges that she was a black separatist and unpatriotic.

A black First Lady is a meaningful and unsettling first. The wording itself is revealing. She is female but *not* white and therefore not the usual "lady". The First Lady is supposed to set the cultural tenor—in clothes, and furnishings, and food, and style. And Michelle has already shown that she can easily do this. She is the *first wife, and first mother, while being* black. The US will have a black mother of the nation. No wonder there was so much anger thrown her way.

Given the history of slavery and racism in the US, black women were not viewed as ladies. With this legacy, they are most often not recognized as mothers either. They have always been depicted more as slaves, or mammies, or domestics, or welfare recipients. It does not matter that Condi Rice is black; or that Michelle is a professional woman with two daughters. Meanwhile, Michelle was tarred with the idea that she calls whites "whitey"—and in the end she was even referred to by Fox News as Obama's babies' mama. Just being First Lady and a black woman unsettles the existing white contours of femininity, motherhood and family.

The unique thing challenging whether or not Michelle was considered to be First Lady material was her color. Otherwise, she fulfilled all the requirements. However, no one, not even the right wing, can say that she is not an appropriate First Lady simply because she is black. Instead, she is made suspect and demonized: militantly black, angry, and not (white)-wifely. She became an important conduit for making Obama less electable. It did not work.

Remember, Michelle was the one wearing the gun on the *New Yorker* cover. Actually, Barack did not need the gun because he was depicted as Muslim: given the Bush–Cheney surround, just being Muslim makes one inappropriate, unpatriotic, worrisome, a terrorist. Or as Hamid Dabashi related to me: as a Muslim he needn't be particularly militant to be problematic, just being Muslim is problem enough. Together, Michelle as black militant woman and Barack as Muslim man spoke the fears of white America.

Although race and gender are almost always inseparable, for women of color they sometimes are experienced in singular and punishing fashion. When I read that Michelle's Princeton roommate's mother asked to have her daughter moved to another room when she found out Michelle was black, I thought that this was an instance that is all about race. The request was completely about Michelle being black and not about her gender. Girls room with girls.[1] Michelle's race appeared once again in singular fashion while she was being considered for First Lady. She obviously had the right sex and gender for this position. It was just her race, and the racialized forms of her gender, that posed a potential problem.

This leads to an interesting comparison between Michelle and Hillary, before Hillary ran for president. They both were lawyers, talented and smart. Both supported their husband's candidacy for president. Hillary, at that time, was a first—a professional woman who did not apologize for her independence and skill. There was a lot of criticism then of Hillary for being non-traditional, and too professional. Michelle's challenge was different. It was/is her race, and her raced gender, not her vision of gender *per se* that was at issue. Given this, Michelle may be as much of a challenge, though differently so, for the White House as if Hillary had become president. This is because Michelle is black, and because Hillary is (white) female. My point may not be easily true because race and gender are neither readily separable nor decipherable from each other. But this comparison is something to think more about.

Michelle as First Lady is already a force of her own. She knows how to be effective and productive. Barack attests to Michelle's dexterity in his autobiography, *The Audacity of Hope*, which I read during the campaign. When he describes himself as trying to do better with assisting with the children he writes about offering to help with Sasha's birthday party. Michelle tells him to get 20 balloons, enough pizza for 20, and ice. He then offers to do more, and handle the goody bags. Michelle assures him that he can't handle the goody bags.[2] I laughed out loud. Here is the next president of the US and I am also sure that the goody bags might just be his undoing.

Misogyny, in its racialized history, was used to smear Michelle Obama in the early stages of her public story. She appeared to those who dislike or fear her as an inauthentic woman (read: not white) and as an authentic black (read: with a chip on her shoulder). She was made out to be too independent, too radical, and too sexual—not white enough. And this meant that she did not have one of the former necessities for being First Lady: being white. Post-election, this no longer is true.

It may be, in the long run, that Michelle is more of a sure bet for the change that Obama's campaign promised than Barack himself. She won't be making policy, as he is, but she has changed the color of who is in charge of the White House, as home of the nation. All this is not just about Michelle Obama the person. It is about the institution of the First Lady who earlier stood in for the white nation. Michelle has unsettled and disturbed this racialized history. If the US is lucky, maybe she will reinvent the nation in new ways by doing so.

As First Lady, Michelle has in some form been automatically domesticated. She follows in the footsteps of what First Ladies, as wives and mothers, have done before. But all the former First Ladies have had the privileges of whiteness's traditional forms of motherhood and wifely status. This allowed them a certain kind of pedestal status that black women have not known. Therefore, whatever Michelle does with the office of First Lady it will be newly altered.

Given black women's history from slavery to the labor force, Michelle's public embrace of her motherhood is in part newly unique. She was an avid participant in the presidential campaign while repeatedly making clear to the public that her two young daughters were her top priority. She told us that they are who she thinks of first when she wakes for the day; and who she thinks of last at the end of it. Michelle's First Lady narrative may become a newly welcomed story that resonates with wage-earning working mothers of all colors.

Michelle also seems instrumental in personalizing Barack's

administration by blurring the lines between the White House and the public domain. She visits soup kitchens and schools and breaks ground for an organic garden on the White House lawn. She makes herself approachable—by carving out this new middle ground. She familiarizes her family through publicized settings of newly located domestic locations. She paints a new palette for herself and maybe women of all colors.

I still remain uncomfortable with the way Barack defers to Michelle about all things domestic and depends on her for their family's nurturance. Too much of this is not new. Yet I hope that Michelle finds new gender possibilities and stretches them outward for us all. As Michelle unsettles and settles the nation as a black mother and wife, I look for her to give birth to a new promissory.

Notes

1   This issue has recently become more complicated as transgendered individuals find themselves in unwanted same-sex arrangements on college campuses.

2   Barack Obama, *The Audacity of Hope* (New York: Three Rivers Press, 2006), p. 349.

17

Sarah's Right-wing Vagina

Republican vice-presidential nominee Sarah Palin became an overnight sensation and celebrity of sorts.

The Republicans, after September 11, 2001, had used the mantra of women's rights to defend their bombing of Afghanistan and Iraq. The Republican Party then next used Palin like a suicide bomber of sorts. Given the outdated and punishing policies of the Bush/Cheney years and McCain's complicity in them, when women suffered the most both in the US and abroad, it was especially galling that the Republicans once again used a female body as their cover-up. And it was newly troubling, especially to progressive feminists of all varieties, to see gender (in the form of Palin) used to trump race (in the form of Obama) as the newer, more poignant agent of change. More psychically—the white cunt was poised against the black phallus.

Palin's candidacy mocked feminism, however it is defined. She might have been an agent of change, but backwards towards anti-"choice" mommy politics. People in the US were told that our nation is secular, and non-extremist, and that the war of/on "terror" stands against religious zealotry. Yet the right wing of the Republican Party made their Christian God the center of patriarchal politics at their presidential convention. Sarah Palin happily conveyed the message in racialized gender decoy form. She was the new "great white hope". She brought God's message. She spoke of the doors that God had cracked open for her. She said she would continue to look for new doors to pass through until the 2012 election.

Supposedly Palin's nomination was to offer former Hillary supporters solace. Palin was presented as an alternative to those women who wanted to see a female on the ticket, any ticket. Yet

Palin was not a self-evidently acceptable exchange. Hillary was more formidable, and more knowledgeable, and even though deeply religious herself more inclusively secular. McCain had gotten this gender "thing" all wrong.

Gender in white skin was supposed to trump race in black skin. So Palin could have five children and look modern and new in a way that no black woman, not even Michelle, could. Racial stereotypes were switched and Michelle and Barack were made to look elitist, and "white" so to speak, with just two, not five, charming children. Sarah was the new rage. At this point in the election Barack faded for a bit, and eyes shifted to the Republican ticket.

Palin made fun of Obama's community organizing—read as urban racial decay. She was mean-spirited and dismissive while parading as a devout Christian woman. Her husband Todd was presented as a man's man, snowmobile champion and good father. There was lots of gender switching and changing while race (being black) and multiculturalism were sidelined as old news.

Manipulations of the meanings of economic class were also integral to Palin's mediated depiction. The Palins' "working"-class roots were manipulated to democratize the Republicans. Todd Palin has a union job and works on oil rigs on the North Slope and can fix a furnace. Palin said she can fix Washington.

It was maddening that the Republican convention—Palin's coming-out party—was such a fabricated event that dismissed the issues that are so crucial to people's survival. Instead, McCain made up an *un*real, *super*real, and *hyper*real s/hero. Mirage displaced everything else. The smoke and mirrors of Sarah's story required an expensive entourage of dress designers, hairstylists, makeup specialists, and so forth. When she accepted her nomination for Vice President she was dressed to the nines, looking fabulous. She presented her right-wing feminist agenda silently but while flirting. She offered her recent pregnancy in coded fashion while holding her infant son. She spoke her avid anti-abortion stance with her pregnant teenage daughter by her side, without needing to say a word. Palin's maverick message read: the more children the merrier.

Palin had made her name in right-wing religious circles as a formidable female politician long before she burst onto the national stage. Although she had not been a key player in the mainstream of the Republican Party, she had significant connections in its religiously extremist wing. She had been grooming for a bigger political stage for a considerable while. In other words, Palin did not happen unexpectedly, nor come from nowhere. She was a well-tuned weapon waiting to be activated. Two well-known Republican conservatives—William Kristol and Dick Morris, who are a part of the long-established Washington elite—were strong backers of Palin's VP nomination. She actively and successfully wooed both of them. They became and continue to be ardent supporters.[1]

Because sex is intimately connected to gender, and gender to race, it is easy for political discourse to manipulate and abuse these relations. As such, Palin was able to construct and parade herself as a faux democrat—the everyday woman as hockey mom. Her female body was used to obfuscate the facts: that she is against abortion in all cases, against sex education in the schools, believes in premarital sexual abstinence and, when that does not work, early marriage. Forget that there are statistics to prove that none of these policy stances are viable, or that your chances of making something of yourself and your child diminish greatly if you are a teen mother.

Instead the Republicans marketed Palin as a woman who would crash the glass ceiling, while paying no attention to the problems of teen mothers who will be unable to crash much that would improve their or their children's lives. Instead of crashing the glass ceiling for women, Palin *is* the glass ceiling for pro-choice women and girls.

McCain's choice of Palin was thought to be a brilliant move on his part until she began to implode. She is young, energetic, sexy, pretty, and politically savvy.[2] Her right-wing credentials—she believes in creationism, is against abortion even in cases of rape and incest, thinks that global warming is not a human-made problem, and so on—would give him legitimacy with disgruntled members of his party. She looks new and bold even though her political/religious zealotry is hardened and crusty, similar to her running mate's persona.

It should not be forgotten that Palin was chosen for VP by the Republican Party in spite of the anti-women plank that she and McCain both endorsed. McCain's record against the Equal Pay Act and for a constitutional amendment against abortion exposed the contradictoriness of this kind of vagina politics—that any (white) vagina is as good as another. Actually, the biological reductionism did not play well. Women and men alike recognized the difference between a pit bull with lipstick and a candidate properly vetted for election.

A cursory comparison between Palin and Clinton reveals the absurdity of the Republican ticket. Palin might have been a breakthrough candidate of sorts, but with none of the experience needed. Palin is no Hillary. They both have vaginas but their policy commitments seriously differ. Hillary might not be feminist enough for me, but she upholds the legal standing of Roe v. Wade. Though she has a faulty foreign policy record, she at least knows that Africa is a continent.

Yet in other ways as well Hillary is no Sarah. Palin is younger, and feisty, and has moxie. She was raised in a post-Title IX world, which gave new sports opprtunities to school girls. She runs marathons, has birthed five babies and looks great, and clearly likes and feels comfortable in her body. She is a new breed of post-boomer white right-wing Republican woman. Hillary is not post-much.

When news anchor Katie Couric first asked Palin if she was a feminist, Sarah said, yes. She believed in women's rights. But a few days later she reversed this position and said she did not like political labels, nor does she need them. Interesting that she is so keen to label her opponents socialist, and terrorist, and un-patriotic.

Regardless of her rejection of the term "feminism", she often spoke of women needing to get a fair shake. She also often said that she hoped to break the glass ceiling for women. She also continually flirted with the crowds as a regular, everyday hockey mom who likes guns. She easily assumed the air of celebrity. It was harder for her to seem viable, if needed, as president.

Although much has been made of Palin's lack of knowledge and experience, it seems only fair to point out that her lack of international experience was the same as George Bush's when he first ran for president. Neither had been to Asia, Africa or South America at the time of their candidacies. Yet nothing could cover over the fact that Palin was strikingly unprepared to hold office. A bit of misogyny, anybody?

The 2008 election very often mimicked reality TV. Celebrities were created and manufactured for the audience by both parties. Obama was elected and Palin hurriedly began a remake of herself . She vied for national exposure from Alaska. Wherever you looked, she was on TV. She wanted to speak for herself. She wanted to prove she was not a diva. She did not ask for the $150,000 wardrobe. She buys her clothes at a downtown thrift store. She drives herself to work without a chauffeur. She cooks dinner for her children. She is a hard-working average American mom.

Hillary and Palin have changed things a bit for women of similar economic means.[3] Wealthy women have the opportunity to run for office and there is not much extraordinary about this any longer. Hillary may have been too wonkish, and Palin not wonkish enough, but they have normalized white females as political candidates for the nation.

The next step is to move beyond opportunity, to equality. Or is it? I think not. This route is not the one I have in mind.

Notes

1   Jane Mayer, "The Insiders", *New Yorker*, October 27, 2008, pp. 38–42.
2   JoAnn Wypijewski, "Beauty and the Beast", *The Nation*, vol. 287, no. 9 (September 29, 2008), p.6
3   Katha Pollitt, "Sayonara, Sarah", *The Nation*, vol. 287, no. 17 (November 24, 2008), p. 11.

18

US Feminisms
....

It's September 2008 and the Democratic primary battles have finally resolved themselves after all the rancor. Hillary and Barack will begin their unity tour shortly. At this moment—after Barack has won the nomination and with Hillary and her supporters still anguished—it is crucial to ask exactly what it is that should be unified here.

Supposedly Barack needs to court and then bring on board Hillary's women. But her followers are actually a pretty homogeneous groups exclusive of many other kinds of women: anti-racist white feminists, Islamic and Muslim and Arab feminists, black feminists, radical sex-feminists, gay rights activists, and so forth. What is needed is a broadly based unity—of the polyversal kind—that recognizes the multiple and diverse varieties of women and their feminisms. Barack is no stranger to this concept, and yet he does not speak of it often enough.

When Maureen Dowd wrote of Hillary's "rabid feminist supporters" she did no one any favors. And when WomenCount PAC, a pro-Hillary political action committee, took out a full-page ad in the *New York Times* stating "not so fast ... Hillary's voice is OUR voice, and she's speaking for all of us"... well, I said, no she is not. The ad continued by stating "we are the women of this nation ... we love our country ... We want Hillary to stay in this race until every vote is cast...". The "we" is problematic because it primarily represents a white feminism that does not embrace racial diversity but rather ignores it. Hillary's campaign, with an assist from media journalists and newscasters, appropriated and colonized feminism in its homogenized, mainstreamed form. I wanted to imagine, and hoped, that an inclusive and progressive anti-racist feminism could become the heart and soul of the remainder of Barack's 2008 campaign.

After Barack won the Democratic nomination, Hillary waited for a while before making her concession speech to her supporters. At the point of conceding, she addressed her constituency as though it were all white. She spoke of her/their glass ceiling. Black women supporters were ignored in terms of the racial victory that had just been won. She spoke about the importance of her breaking the gender barrier, but there was no direct mention of Barack's breaking the racial barrier. Instead, she said more indirectly that "together they achieved milestones". I wish Hillary could have said that Obama's win was a win for all women in the struggle for (racial) equality but she did not. She could have said that his win was a triumph for all of us, but she did not. As such, the race/gender divide was left in place.

Hillary's campaign slowly, even if contradictorily, developed a (white) feminist consciousness. Many women in this country embraced Hillary as a female before she embraced them. By the time she delivered her concession speech, she readily said that she wanted women to have "equality of opportunity, equal pay, and equal respect". She asked for an end to all prejudices in the US. She spoke about her glass ceiling and the 16 million cracks it had now suffered. When all is said and done, however, Barack needs to be careful not to reproduce Hillary's race/gender divide. He needs to be careful what cues he takes from Hillary if the polyglot racial identities of women are to be recognized.

Yes, Hillary has grit and fortitude, but most women *have* to have this grit to make their lives and their families work today. Many men do too. Most people are working harder than ever and not achieving more. The American Dream is in a shambles as people just try to find the money for food and gas. So please, Barack, could you stop saying that Hillary has changed the world that our daughters will live in. The everyday lives of women and girls are what most people dream to change, not becoming president.

Hillary is a power-filled woman who has run for president, and some have mistakenly interpreted this as making her a spokesperson for "women". She used much of the agenda of the white mainstream women's movement of the 1970s and politically activated some remnants of this movement. But it holds women back to resort to the old cliché of liberal feminism: work hard and you can achieve any of your dreams. Many feminists, especially black feminists such as bell hooks, Barbara Smith, and Beverly Guy-Sheftall, never embraced this agenda to begin with. Barack needs to listen and recognize that Hillary does not speak in all of "our names".

Barack rolled out his woman's agenda as a lead-up to the "unity" event in New Hampshire with Hillary. He celebrated Title IX and what it has done for girls and women in sports today. He spoke of his two young daughters, Sasha and Malia, and his wish that they have the same opportunities as any boy. He called for equal pay for women with men. He spoke on behalf of easing the tensions and demands on working women and extending the Family and Medical Leave Act. All to the good, but there are both old and new ways to articulate women's polyversal needs that still need attention.

Barack should learn from US black feminists who have argued clearly that race and gender issues cannot be separated; that equal pay is not sufficient if there are racialized/engendered ghettos in the labor force that disproportionately limit all women, but especially women of color, to low-pay jobs to begin with. Equal pay for low-pay jobs is not enough.

Some women are now accomplished athletes, doctors, and lawyers, but many more are home health aides, and waitresses, and service workers. Many of these low-pay workers are most newly women of color from around the globe. Feminisms of many kinds recognize the newest meanings of global patriarchy. Given this, old feminist formulations may still be necessary, but are also insufficient. New understandings of sex, gender, and race in their global formulations are still needed.

As long as women are disproportionately responsible for domestic labor and child care, focusing on equal wages, though urgently necessary, is not enough. As long as the sexual division of labor demands that a majority of women have double and triple days of labor—domestic, childrearing, and waged—women are not free to become equal, so to speak. They are simply free to work very, very hard. Barack has recognized that there needs to be a new politics of race today. He has yet to recognize fully the newest politics of gender.

Progressive feminists seek a platform that recognizes that *all* women are working hard and that family and work is a false divide; that equal pay is a human right but hardly complete. Feminists of all differing identities—black, Asian, Islamic, Arab, and so on—also share a unified hope that wars across the globe will end, and economic budgets will be rebuilt that focus on affordable/available health care, better schools, more available day care, and new roads and bridges.

Feminisms today recognize the need for female-specific policies that also claim the shared and varied identities of all people. Women's specific needs for pregnancy leave are understood as connected to a myriad of larger inclusive issues that affect all people. Each human being is both similar and different to another being. Feminists of all sorts get it.

Maybe one of the most significant things about the 2008 election is that it brought the complexity of feminisms to the fore of mainstream politics. At the start of the primary process it looked like Hillary would win the nomination. But that was before, before women of all colors, including white women, chose Barack. And it was before women rejected Palin as an acceptable stand-in for Hillary. The simple equation of female bodies, complex gender and racial identities, and a homogeneous (white) feminism was debunked for the entire globe to see.

It is hopeful that the first important bill to be signed by Obama in his second week in office was the Lilly Ledbetter Fair Pay Act. This bill rewrites the statute of limitations on women filing pay discrimination complaints against their employers and gives them a shot at the equal pay they deserve. The signing also acknowledged the many women who supported Hillary and then later supported his candidacy. But Barack needs to go still further and acknowledge other feminisms that believe that equal pay is just a start at equity. And that racialized and gendered ghettos in the labor market also must be recognized and removed. Maybe Michelle will help here.

The US presidential campaign had the potential to clarify the power of anti-racist feminisms in all their glorious plural variations. Feminisms shift and change with the world. And the world shifts and changes alongside the structures of race and gender and class. We—the inclusive "we"— must keep our ears to the ground and our eyes to the sky to find and create new radically anti-racist feminisms for this next century.

Shifting the
Political Landscapes

19

Gender Mainstreaming in the Land of Picasso

I traveled to Barcelona in spring 2006, and to Paris in spring 2007 before the US presidential primaries had begun. My conversations and thoughts from these travels resonated loudly while I was in Sweden in the fall of 2008, after Obama had won the Democratic nomination. Women's lives were speedily changing, and also remaining agonizingly stagnant. In some sense my visit to the Picasso Museum in Paris just before delivering an address titled "Globalization and Sexual Decoys" was all too poignant. Picasso's famous drawings of (white) women encase them in their gender with little possibility of escape. I carried his caricatured images of women with me while I spoke about the fluidities and manipulations of gender. But I will return to this.

I went to Barcelona to deliver a keynote address that spoke against the role of US women in making the wars on Afghanistan and Iraq, and to learn more about the mainstreaming of gender in Spanish politics. Women at the *Centre de Cultura de Dones Francesca Bonnemaison* were interested in discussing the difficult process of bringing women into the political arena as "equals" while not allowing misogynist standards to continue to define their participation. To me, Spain appeared to be well ahead of the US in terms of gender equity.

President Jose Luis Zapatero in his first term, in non-masculinist/militarist form, had pulled out all Spanish troops from Iraq, and had appointed equal numbers of men and women, nine each, to his initial cabinet. Interestingly, the nine men had more than twenty children between them, and the women, seven. This unequal equality of sorts still spoke misogynist privilege: each of the men had a wife to oversee family life, and the women did not.

After Zapatero's re-election, his second cabinet was made up of more women than men. His defense minister, Carme Chacon, a self-avowed pacifist, took her oath of office while pregnant, and she continued to oversee the armed forces with her pregnant belly. Spain is also now quite proud of its sweeping laws against domestic violence, its legalization of gay marriage, and its legal commitment to gender parity.

These formal commitments are not one and the same with actual women's equality but they are importantly defiant of existing engendered norms. Gender equality has been noted, and the need for redress has been recognized. It remains to be seen how much female politicians will make a difference as women, for women; as well as whether gender can be successfully mainstreamed into already existing misogynist structures and dislocate patriarchal privilege. Females as elected officials challenge the notion that politicians must be male. But what this gender destabilization fully means for most "ordinary" women remains to be seen.

It is not at all clear that one can summarily assume that all females will make the same gender difference. Many feminists across the globe think that the appointment of the South African jurist and grassroots activist Navanethem Pillay as UN High Commissioner for Human Rights offers a promise of significant change. She has worked her way up from the bottom, struggling for women and their rights; she then became an important participant in the Rwandan tribunals that defined rape as a crime of war. Her early ties to women's struggles that existed outside the mainstream resonate with new possibility in comparison with women politicians who are groomed from inside.

Zapatero's government has received and mobilized substantial support from a range of women's activists and feminists for his gender mainstreaming. There are activist liberal feminist types in the socialist party who stand firmly for equality doctrine—meaning sameness of treatment—as well as socialist feminists who wish for a more complex reading of equity. In discussions in Barcelona I realized that an activist liberal feminist approach that demands equality, although too narrow in scope, is much more probing and useful than the US neoliberal feminist individualism and opportunity doctrine that dominated during the Bush/Cheney years.

During my stay in Barcelona I had a first-hand look at what gender mainstreaming could look like for "ordinary", everyday people. Vertical steps in the hillsides and at entries to the metro were being replaced by new walkways and cemented paths to make them "women-friendly". These changes meant that women, or men, with shopping carts and baby carriages would be able to navigate the city more easily. At the same time that these reforms change women's lives they also make the subways accessible to disabled persons, and/or anyone dragging or pushing a shopping cart.

Attempts at gender mainstreaming have been inconsistent and incomplete, and yet when accomplished they most often open new possibilities. These changes take isolating aspects of the responsibilities and necessities of private life and incorporate them more easily into everyday public life. Gender mainstreaming identifies and strategizes gender as part of each and every policy design and implementation. It integrates gender by normalizing the discourse, and/or practice, by full and total inclusion.[1]

While in Barcelona I wondered whether it was not better to regender the mainstream, rather than mainstream the gender. Many feminists in Spain, like the Chilean Judith Astelerra, think that by doing the latter, the former will come. She also believes that by explicitly attacking gender bias, the bias will be removed. There is continual monitoring to enhance the success of mainstreaming gender. Audits are conducted to measure the "efficiency of implementation" of equal opportunity policies and goals. However, the problem that remains is also the promise: that by changing formal structures, informal inequalities will be redressed. This assumes that women can and will make this difference.

Not too long before my trip to Barcelona, Michele Bachelet was elected president of Chile. She, a survivor of torture and imprisononment, and then a Minister of Defense, had long opposed the Chilean dictatorship of Augusto Pinochet. She had standing in her country as a former defender, along with her father, of socialist president Salvador Allende. Women voted for her by a 5 percent margin even though she is not some one who came from organized feminist politics. Nevertheless, she spoke as a strong supporter of women's education and women's rights. Her legacy is still being written. As several women politicians said to me in Barcelona: if you are in the government, you have to "do" what governments do. While feminists on the outside of government are said to be ineffectual, mainstreamers say they are inside, doing professional politics, and eventually will make a difference.

Similar discussions and critical inquiries were evident during my visit to Paris in March 2007 for the international symposium "Gender at the Heart of Globalization", held at the Ministère de la Recherche. I presented my thoughts about how gender fluidity allows for and initiates multiple meanings that can create gender decoys of a particular kind. In other words, that there are many kinds of women parading as female, or many female bodies parading as women. And this dislocates the very notion of woman as a homogenous category at the start.

My stance complicates the more static notion of gender for the purposes of mainstreaming. As women occupy differentiated gender constructs it is less easy to assume that when you switch the sex you necessarily switch the gender. A female soldier must kill like a male one. A female military officer must follow militarist logic.

Similar queries followed me to Orebro, Sweden, in September, 2008, at the international conference "The War Question for Feminism", which focused especially on women's positioning and mainstreaming in the military and in wars across the globe. Most of the presentations queried whether women can be treated fairly and equally in militarized situations. Militarism itself was not interrogated— and nor was the necessity of war.

Sweden has its own interesting historical context to reckon with. Its women were an early part of the labor force in the 1970s, given Sweden's rapid expansion of the public sector. Later Swedish women continued in the public sphere, due in part to restrictive immigration policies. Yet progressive policy initiatives of state-supported day care and family leave policies developed out of this situation. And complex relations of race and gender appeared while immigration restrictions and discrimination against immigrants also allowed progress for white middle-class Swedish women. Swedish men were also positioned as the good guys compared to the "othered" foreigners, especially Muslim men. Meanwhile Swedish men have also gained from these equal status policies while women continue to do four times as much of the domestic labor.

The complexities of legal equality in Sweden are further noted by Maud Eduards as she describes the problematic aspects of identical treatment on military peacekeeping missions that require same-use practices of toilets and showers. Such perfect equity actually dissuades women from joining and participating in military missions. A few of us at the conference wondered whether female participation in militarized zones and war is a laudatory goal to begin with, but this remained more off the table for critique than on.

Equality, at the conference proceedings, was assumed to mean sameness of treatment even though there are differences between male and female bodies; and even though there are social, political, economic, and racial inequalities that are gendered. Universal, meaning unitary and singular, directives are insufficient. It is why I use the term poly/versal rather than uni/versal. *Poly* represents the variety of specific selves; and *versal* speaks to the connectedness of the variety that cuts across and through gender. *Uni* envisions equity as equivalent to oneness.

It is important to recognize that Islamic feminisms do not equate equality with sameness. Nor do African American feminists, who have long suffered their "difference" of race and gender. Females are instead understood to be commonly different and differently common; and similarly different and differently similar to each other, and to men.[2] The dichotomized formulation: same *or* different is not helpful. Neither is the notion that there are only two genders, or that gender concerns are Western, and/or white.

There have long been other-than-Western-and-white feminists across the globe—of every type and variety—that argued and continue to argue that women's equality is a problematic and insufficient goal. Instead of equality with men, which already assumes a heteronormative engendered and racialized hierarchy, women need liberation from these hierarchical standards. Sadly, these equality demands have become more radical today—given neoliberal assaults on all forms of equality across the globe.

Because of these assaults and limits I encouraged and supported much of the on-going on-the-ground activity that many of the participants at the conference spoke of, especially their support for UN Resolution 1325 which argues for "increased representation of women at all decision-making levels in national, regional and international institutions and mechanisms for the prevention, management, and resolution of conflict". At the same time that this resolution is important to use as a guide for demanding needed change, it is insufficient to use in isolation. Instead, women's activism must aggressively support radicalized women's movements that are not limited to the structural confines of established and mainstreamed politics.

In my keynote address at the Swedish conference I argued that women's involvement and participation in war are deeply troubling because women have allowed the US to look more democratic, more equal, in a sense, with females making and/or defending our wars, be it Condoleezza Rice or Hillary Clinton. My disparagement of Condi and Hillary was meant to highlight the problem of a non-defiant and non-radically democratic notion of gender.

It was at this conference, where there were many Hillary supporters from afar, that I first realized how much the US feminist tensions of the 2008 primaries could be useful to feminisms, especially Western ones, across the globe. I argued that it was not inevitable that any woman politician could make enough of a progressive difference. Female bodies were insufficient. Vagina politics, be it in the form of a Hillary or a Palin, are not enough.

When I returned home my new *Signs: Journal of Women and Culture in Society* was waiting in my pile of mail. It was uncanny to me that its lead symposium was on "Challenges to Women's Leadership". I read that in the twenty-seven states making up the European Union (EU) there are women presidents in Finland and Ireland and a woman prime minister in Germany, with Finland, Sweden and Spain having between 40 and 50 percent women ministers. The article also stated that in countries that achieved at least 30-plus percent representation of women in elected office, it is difficult to form large coalitions of women to mobilize for greater change.[3]

Najma Chowdhury tells us that the two female prime ministers of Bangladesh, Khaleda Zia and Sheikh Hasina, during the period 1991–2006 did not make a difference in challenging patriarchal values. Neither "possessed gender consciousness"; nor did they "challenge the gender dynamics in society" which are the "touchstones of the women's movement in Bangladesh".[4]

Troung Thi Thuy Hang argues that Vietnam has had "a long tradition of gender equality" and also a long history of gender stratification and structural barriers to parity.[5] Amanda Gouws of South Africa writes that new formal equality law has not created substantive gains for women in spite of an amazing "gender machinery" of "gender desks" in all state departments. The outcome has left South Africa with "no coherent women's movement to mobilize women" to hold "women in government accountable".[6]

Neema Kudva and Kajri Misra advance the nuanced analysis that the use of quotas in India to bring a critical mass of women into government creates new opportunities while also closing them down. The first nationwide elections in 1995 "brought almost eight hundred thousand women into local government" in India. And yet this massive change also has stymied "a broad-based feminist collective agenda" that pushes for "gender justice". Without such a presence quotas remain underdeveloped as a strategy for women's liberation.[7]

The requisites of established politics curtail feminist options at the very same time that disillusionment with established politics pushes more women to get involved in government. And I continue to wonder whether women are more readily able to enter national politics only because it has declined as a location of power. Nevertheless, the nation still negotiates and sets the policies that affect its public and private life. And, then, maybe certain feminist agendas can make a difference, even if not sufficiently so. But this entails switching the gender (woman as such), more than simply switching the sex (female). Biology is not irrelevant here, but also not determinative, because feminist policies may or may not be embraced by a female.

The querying of mainstreaming as a strategy for gender justice must be reviewed in light of the newly new global world of excessive economic inequality. Because women of all colors are disproportionately *still* the poorest of the poor, the mainstreaming may be *more* problematic than it was a decade ago. In other words, the mainstreaming of women into governments and their militaries may allow for the masking of grave economic and racial injustices to the majority of women.

Maybe this institutionalized and demobilized form of gender equity acts like a bailout of its own for misogyny, along with and alongside the bailout of Wall Street. This just might be the newest form of the patriarchal regulatory system in play, protecting the exploitation of most women by legitimizing a few in positions of power. The economic zealotry of global capitalism may have found its newest political articulation in modernized patriarchy: female presidents alongside otherwise gendered inequity.

Let me return to Picasso. On my trip to Paris I visited the Picasso Museum twice. First I viewed his well-known artworks of imaginary/imaged women depicting his somewhat torrid sexual life. His female bodies, always a figuring of multiple breasts, bespeak beauty, ugliness, disharmony, attraction and repulsion as the differing illusions and unspoken fantasies of the male gaze.[8] On my second visit to the museum I viewed the exhibit of Picasso's bullfighting period.

The Spanish bullfighters, and the bulls themselves, were depicted as a variety of penises. Using differing angles and designs Picasso constructed a static, unchanging message of machismo. This phallic venue of the bull-fighting ring and his distorted female bodies posing as gender itself remind us of the unchanging symbols of misogyny.

It is telling that Spain, the same country that gives us gender mainstreaming, also produced Picasso, the greatest Spanish icon—the very new with the very old.

Notes

1   Joan Acker, "Hierarchies, Jobs, Bodies: A Theory of Gendered Organiza-
     tions", *Gender and Society*, vol. 4, no. 2 (June, 1990), pp. 139–158; Judith
     Squires, "Is Mainstreaming Transformative? Theorizing Mainstreaming in
     the Context of Diversity and Deliberation", *Social Politics: International
     Studies in Gender, State and Society*, vol.12, no. 3 (Fall 2005), pp. 366–388;
     Sylvia Walby, *et al.*, ed., *Gendering the Knowledge Economy* (London:
     Palgrave, 2007) and Walby, "Gender Mainstreaming: Productive Tensions
     in Theory and Practice", *Social Politics: International Studies in Gender,
     State and Society*, vol.12, no. 3 (fall 2005), pp. 321–43; and Maria
     Stratigaki, "Gender Mainstreaming vs. Positive Action", *European Journal
     of Women's Studies*, vol. 12, no. 2 (2005), pp. 16–86.
2   See my *The Color of Gender* (Berkeley: University of California Press,
     1994); and *Against Empire* (London: Zed Books, 2004) for a full account
     of these particular feminist articulations.

3   Monique Leyenaar, "Challenges to Women's Political Representation in Europe", *Signs*, vol. 34, no. 1 (Autumn, 2008), pp. 1, 4.

4   Najma Chowdhury, "Lessons on Women's Political Leadership from Bangladesh", *Signs*. vol. 34, no. 1, pp. 8, 11.

5   Truong Thi Thuy Hang, "Women's Leadership in Vietnam: Opportunities and Challenges", *Signs*, ibid., pp. 16, 20.

6   Amanda Gouws, "Obstacles for Women in Leadership Positions: The Case of South Africa", *Signs*, vol. 34, no. 1, pp. 21, 25, 26.

7   Neema Kudva and Kajri Misra, "Gender Quotas, the Politics of Presence, and the Feminist Project: What Does the Indian Experience Tell Us?", *Signs*, vol. 34, no. 1, pp. 49, 68, 69.

8   Jay Bernstein, "The Demand for Ugliness: Picasso's Bodies", paper presented at the Critical Theory Seminar, "Society for the Humanities", Cornell University, Summer, 2008.

20

Chadors, Veils, and Pantsuits

Political struggle is too readily written with and on female bodies. The US has justified and authorized its wars of/on "terror" in the name of women's rights in the countries where it wages war, while destroying the fabric of life for women and girls in those countries. Women in these countries have lost rights, once again, to the Taliban and right-wing clerics. This backdrop of right-wing fanaticism legitimates the secular/religious divide while it also negates its plausibility and viability. The issue of women's dress and veiling becomes a metaphoric device for having a conversation about secularism.

I do not wish to encode the discussion of the veil with further distortion and ignorance, and I risk this by singling it out as an issue to examine. The issue of veiling is embedded in deep prejudices and misunderstandings that ignore the complicated and varied histories of women in Islam. Muslim women's dress expresses differing and also contradictory meanings depending on its particular history of colonial and anti-colonial feminist struggle. There is no singular story or interpretation that is universally true.

The process of de-veiling, unveiling and re-veiling more often than not constructs women in Islam as passive and oppressed. Sometimes, however, these women are not passive and are players in their own choice and fate. Other times, Islamic women have been veiled as a response to their defiance and determination to craft their own lives. In still other circumstances they have been veiled because of the new places they occupy and demand in the public world.

The veil should be seen more as a site of contestation and struggle than of sheer enforced control and its concordant passivity. Historical and cultural specificity must be recognized so that wrong assumptions and parallels are not drawn. There are many veils, chadors, abayyas. The blue burqa—which entirely engulfs the face and body— enforced by the Taliban in Afghanistan should not be wrongly universalized to all veiling practices. As often as not, women in Islam choose or have chosen to wear the veil. Women are never as silenced or passive as they are made to seem, whether Korean, Somalian, Iranian, Turkish, Moroccan, South African, and so on. There are home-grown feminisms to be found everywhere.

Public spaces are usually differentiated from private, personal spaces in countries considered to be modern. Because actions that are taken in public are in view, women in public are surveilled more carefully. Muslim women are the visible location for negotiating the place of acceptable religious practices and their masculinist interpretations, especially in public spaces. As such the veil has often been a prime site for enforced religiosity. The reaction to this cultural imposition is often women's resistance in order to define their own selves.

There are various Islamist and Muslim women's histories and permeable contexts to sort through in Algeria, France, Holland, England, Nigeria, Iran, and Turkey. The multiplicity of meanings attach to the variety of Muslims. Dutch Muslims come from Indonesia, Surinam, Morocco, and Turkey. British Muslims mainly derive from the Indian subcontinent, a lot of these via East Africa (the "Ugandan Asians"), but also from the Maghreb (Saharan Africa), Somalia, Egypt, Turkey, Nigeria, the women observing a mix of dress codes that do not simply reflect either their place of origin or their religion.[1] German Muslims are very often Turks. French Muslims often come from the Maghreb. The struggle over veiling takes place in these host/ immigrant locations. Ayaan Hirsi Ali, the Somali-born Muslim woman who became famously outspoken against Muslim extremism in Amsterdam gave voice to anti-Islamic rhetoric.[2] It is these differing voices that continue the debate over the meaning of women's self-determination and liberation.

Nilufer Gole argues that a non-assimilationist Islam creates tensions for a Europeanized Islam. In France and Holland this tension is focused on the right to veil in public.[3] The struggle to disallow the veil/headscarf attempts to rearticulate the public sphere as "Western" and therefore secular. This notion of secularity supposedly positions non-patriarchal, non-religious practices against Islam and its patriarchal religiosity. For Gole, "no other symbol than the veil reconstructs with such force the 'otherness' of Islam to the West". And, women's body coverings reveal the centrality of the gendered Islamic critique of Western modernity. In Islam "women are makers of modesty and morality" and therefore the gender question elaborates the relationship between Islamism and modernism, and Islamic modernities.[4] There is obviously, then, more than one kind of Islamism and more than one kind of modernity.

Young urban Turkish women use the veil to express "an active modesty" that takes a traditional expression and politicizes it anew in public. During the Turkish Kemalist revolution in 1923, women deveiled as bearers of Westernization and secularism. Today's veiling "turkan movement" of university students uses the headscarf as a discursive symbol embracing women as public citizens with women's rights.[5] The complex uses and abuses of the veil make a headscarf ban falsely homogenizing and essentializing of those who wear it.

Because there is no singular meaning of the headscarf or one agreed-upon meaning of it within Muslim populations it remains an unresolved conflict. This conflict is most clearly depicted in Turkey with its secular state, a formidable Islamist party, and a large number of Islamists favoring "the" headscarf.[6] Self-identifying secularists feared the wearing of the headscarf by Merve Kavakci, deputy of the Islamist Virtue Party, when she was sworn into the national assembly. The contested banning of the headscarf reveals the conflicts and uncertainties and irresolution about women's place in the Muslim public world.

The veil establishes but also unsettles cultural discourses about women's place. Afsaneh Najmabadi argues that the undressing of women—deveiling—readies them for public life, and also from the French viewpoint protects the manliness of the public sphere by keeping it a masculine and gendered space, with no veil. The Western notion of equivalence—that equality means sameness of treatment—is challenged while the public sphere remains a masculinist enclave. Accordingly, the veil becomes a homo-social marker that controls and rationalizes women.[7] The veil regulates and disciplines homo/hetero borders. But it also makes Muslims more publicly visible and "this Islamic presence in public therefore challenges the strict separation between private religion and public secularism".[8]

The secular/religious divide, problematic as it is, was starkly drawn in France in the 2004 debate over its headscarf ban in public schools. The headscarf in this instance reflects issues of race as well as gender: the French stance towards immigrant populations of its former colonies now living within its midst. Historically, when France arrived in Algeria in 1830, it sought to subjugate, "civilize", and modernize the country, according to Joan Scott, by removing the veil worn by Muslim women. Today's wearing of the veil by Muslim women is a rejection of this colonial stance of domination and control.

France responds with laws that demand "assimilation to a singular culture" in an attempt to eradicate "intolerable difference" of the Muslim sort. The French demand their "universal" type of secularism.[9] French citizenship was denied Fadela Amara because of her choosing to wear the niqab, a veil that covers the entire face except the eyes. The denial was justified on the basis of "insufficient assimilation" and the judgment that the niqab was not religious expression but a "totalitarian political project that promotes inequality between the sexes and is totally lacking in democracy".[10]

Muslim feminists and some "believing women" do not use the term "feminist" because of its Western and imperial identity. They, however, fully embrace women's equality. Some, like Asma Barlas, argue that the Qur'an is in fact a radically egalitarian and anti-patriarchal text. She does not accept the defensive posture of Islam, as set against the West, and rather argues for the richly democratic promissory of Islam for women.[11]

Hamid Dabashi argues that Islamic ideology and theology at their best constitute a militant voice of democratic discontent that has been distorted by the false dichotomy: Islam vs. the West. This oppositional stance has silenced the multifocal, multi-local, multivocal and cosmopolitan roots of Islam. This optimal Islamic ideology is then a mix of both Islam and the West, that de-essentializes Islam and re-envisions the West, leaving neither what it was.[12] These more complex contexts defining the veil are not seen or heard much in the West.

Instead the Bush/Cheney administration designed the war on/of "terror" against the "Islamic terrorist threat" and the "backwardness" of "Islam's" women. So I think it is really interesting to think about the differing ways cultures "veil" and constrain women. Hillary Clinton competed against Barack Obama for the presidential nomination of their party while wearing pantsuits each and every day. Her body was covered and "veiled" so to speak, but in Western fashion. She is talented, and powerful, and yet remained constrained by her body.

She and many professional Western women try to be careful not to call attention to their sensuality or their female body parts in order not to unsettle the normalized expectations of public space. The pantsuit became Hillary's signature garment. The pantsuit is often the West's notion of appropriate female modesty. It symbolizes a woman treading carefully in a "man's" world. Carefully means astutely, and cautiously.

Some may say that Hillary and other professional types just wear what they like to wear, and this may be so. And, yet, maybe the pantsuit is worn because Hillary has legs she wants to hide.

Some might say that pantsuits are, anyway, so yesterday. There obviously are many possibilities and interpretations.

However, the fact that Hillary *always* wears pants says more about Western misogyny than any of us would like to admit. And it says as much about how our misogynistic culture dresses women as it says about how Islam uses the veil.

Notes

1   Thanks to my copy-editor, Pat Harper, for this point.

2   Ayaan Hirsi Ali, *Infidel* (New York: Free Press, 2007).

3   Nilufer Gole, "Islam Resetting the European Agenda?", *Public Culture*, vol. 18, no. 1 (2006), p. 11.

4   Nilufer Gole, *The Forbidden Modern Civilization and Veiling* (Ann Arbor: University of Michigan Press, 1996), pp. 1, 4. Also see Nilufer Gole, "Snapshots of Islamic Modernities", *Daedalus*, vol. 129, no. 1 (Winter, 2000), p. 103.

5   Ibid., *The Forbidden Modern*, pp. 4, 14, 84.

6   Yesim Arat, "One Ban and Many Headscarves: Islamist Women and Democracy in Turkey", *International Social Science Review*, vol. 2, no. 1 (2001), pp. 47, 58.

7   Afsaneh Najmabadi, *Women with Mustaches and Men Without Beards* (Berkeley: University of California Press, 2005), pp. 133, 135, 155.

8   Nilufer Gole, "Islam, European Public Space and Civility", www.eurozine.com, May 3, 2007.

9   Joan Wallach Scott, *Politics of the Veil* (Princeton: Princeton University Press, 2007), pp. 12, 31, 45, 46, 55.

10 Katrin Bennhold, "A Veil Closes France's Door to Citizenship", *New York Times*, July 18, 2008, p. A1.

11 Asma Barlas, *Believing Women in Islam* (Austin: University of Texas, 2002).

12 Hamid Dabashi, *Islamic Liberation Theology* (New York: Routledge, 2008), pp. x, 168, 490.

21

New Turkish and Iranian Feminisms

Women in most countries have defied and transcended the prescribed boundaries of gender, both historically and contemporarily. Historical and political memory has silenced this truth. At present, important new formulations of feminisms have developed out of the historical necessities of the wars of/on "terror" and the advance of global capitalism's newest demand for women's labor.[1] Women continue to provide the labor that they always have and are now also a new massive consumer market that puts them center stage. Amidst these developments, I am intrigued by the misrepresentation by mainstream global media of feminisms in Muslim countries as either Western and therefore liberal feminist, or Islamic and therefore non-secular, non-liberally democratic.

Some women in Islamic countries offer Islamic alternatives to misogynistic practices. Other varieties of feminism offer the more established Western discourse of universal rights and gender equality based on sameness of treatment of the sexes. There is more connection between these different types than usually thought. If sameness and difference are not understood as polar opposites, and rather a notion of similarity replaces the notion of sameness, then equivalence can absorb notions of difference and singularity. In other words, same and similar are not equivalent in meaning. Similar treatment allows for differences.

Turkish women are embroiled in democratic struggles even while Islamic extremists attempt to dominate the political agenda and 99 percent of Turkey is Muslim. Debates rage over the meaning of the wearing of the headscarf in public places while women's rights agendas take second place. The Turkish state supplicates for entry to the Economic Union by holding forth with the "secular" mantra. Meanwhile, a Westernized Turkey ratified CEDAW (the Convention on the Elimination of All Forms of Discrimination Against Women) which insured a commitment to female literacy, while the Islamist Welfare Party became part of the ruling coalition in 1995.

Turkish "secular" women organized to stand against the push for headgear while the coalition government de-emphasized the Beijing human rights approach and opted for cultural specificity. Today there are women's groups, like Women Against Sharia, who protest the Welfare Party's attack on women in public life. Their demonstrations bring hundreds of thousands of women onto the streets.[2] Turkish women are once again the site of the battleground for establishing a separation between Islamic fundamentalism and the West. This may be so despite the troublesome efficacy of the divide, and maybe because of it.

If the construct and conception of women's rights are not given over to and appropriated by the West then they are not normalized in opposition to Islamic practices. There are many Islams. Modern Islam does not automatically or necessarily deny recognition to their kind of feminisms. In 2004, Turkish women demonstrated holding signs reading: "Our Bodies and Sexuality Belong to Ourselves". As often as not, Islamic authoritarian and totalizing conceptions of traditional gender identities along with Western universalisms are rejected in favor of women's plurality and need for choice.[3]

Afsaneh Najmabadi argues for a radicalized Iranian feminism: that Iranian feminists need to embolden themselves further and embrace sexual "others", meaning male homosexuality and same-sex affectivity. She rejects the construction that equates heterosexuality with modernity and the modern; rather she shows a history that is disciplining of masculinity as hetero, and not homo. For her, gender is not the "male/female binary that we now take for granted". The pre-modern golden age was one of multiple sexualities. Only historical amnesia creates the eradication of male homoeroticism and the blurring of gender lines.[4]

Homosexuality is denied by and prosecuted in many Muslim states. Interestingly, in Iran homosexuality is punishable by death but sex-change operations are legal. Such a seeming contradiction is resolved by the initial acceptance of gender differentiation. These biological alterations continue the practice of gender differentiation within a heteronormative paradigm.[5] Homosexuality on the other hand more readily challenges the entirety of this binary framework.

More mainstreamed, although often persecuted in Iran, are women's rights activists. The historical processes of patriarchal domination, the needs of global capital, and radical clerics' attempt to control and regulate traditional modes of gender have defined Iranian women's lives. In the 1920s Reza Shah attempted to Westernize Iran and strip clerics of their power, particularly over women. Unveiling women, in this instance, became part of a liberatory state policy. Throughout Iranian history there have been mixed and varied feelings among women about their enfranchisement and recognition.

As Iranian women, mainly married women, throughout the 1970s entered the labor force, especially as health workers and secretaries, the veil was donned less. This practice of unveiling was also an aspect of Shah Pahlavi's US-supported regime that the 1979 Islamic revolution led by Khomeini sought to challenge. The Islamic revolution promised a "true recognition of women" with "new gender identity" from what the Western-identified Pahlavi demanded. Khomeini mobilized women for the revolution against Western imperialism and then re-veiled them through his newly established clerical control.[6] Women who had supported him felt betrayed by this reversal.[7]

For Ziba Mir-Hosseini, Iran has its own form of indigenous feminism that derives in and with the struggle with sharia (Islamic law). She holds sharia accountable to its own tenets of "justice and equality" and argues that these commitments must guide the attack against second-class citizenship of women. She uses Islamic law as her guide and pre-requisite to women's equality, not Western feminism. Those who speak of the holy texts must admit that the laws derived from them are a matter of human interpretation. "The prevailing interpretations of the sharia do not reflect the values and principles that I hold to be at the core of my faith."[8]

Many Iranian feminists, like the religious Islamic women called the "talabeh", believe that they are modern and autonomous and not submissive. Wearing their veils, talabeh women demand the modernization of religious practices.[9] They see the chador as both traditional and non-traditional; they argue that the hijab has been imposed and not, and that when the veil was politicized at first in the Revolution it gave public voice to women. Most recently, highly educated *chadori* (women who wear the chador) pose a threat to traditional Islamic patriarchy as they demand a voice in once-masculine religious enclaves.

Given the wars of/on "terror", along with the newest demands of the global economy, it makes perfect sense that Islamic feminisms should be a part of the global discourses about misogyny and women's lives. The excesses of global capital stretch and pull at gender borders and do so more particularly in countries that are newly drawn into consumer as well as labor markets. As a result, women are more mobile and expect later marriages and fewer pregnancies than their mothers.

According to Norma Claire Moruzzi and Fatemeh Sadeghi, in Iran "gender inequality has evolved into specifically modern forms: sexual harassment on the street, gender discrimination in the workplace and the sexual double standard in the bedroom". They believe that young Iranian women "balance their individual gender identity on a knife edge of approbation and dismay". They reject traditional Islamic patriarchal authority but have yet to develop a fully developed "indigenous modern conception of feminine power". As a consequence they suffer gender inequality in a new form: "the right of the woman to be held accountable for her own relative lack of power".[10]

The secular/Islamic binary distorts the complex discussion of Iranian feminisms. As Golbarg Bashi writes: "the Iranian women's rights movement is in a predicament. It is still very much an urban and middle-class, Persian-speaking movement, which is fragmented and also heavily censored by officials of the Islamic Republic. It functions today within a system of gender apartheid and its gains are therefore painstakingly slow." She sees the most recent demonstrations by Iranian women as proof of the gradual rise of a women's rights movement that goes beyond other reformist politics but is also at great risk from the Iranian regime of Ahmadinejad. His intolerant rule was easily used by the Bush/Cheney regime to demonize Iran, and smother the small space that exists in Iran for a democratic agenda for women.

These developments are at great cost to the women and feminists in Iran. For Bashi, it is the Iranian women's movement that is the boldest manifestation on the Iranian political landscape. She believes that a transformative women's rights movement that is inclusive of all peoples and religions is possible if the religious/modern dyad is not allowed to dominate. And she is deeply saddened at the arrests on March 12, 2007 and solitary confinement of women's rights activists Shadi Sadr and Mahboubeh Abasgholizadeh, charged with being a threat to national security. They initiated the Stop Stoning Forever Campaign and support the campaign of One Million Signatures to Change the Discriminatory Law. Bashi argues that these Iranian women's activists need support from feminists of all types, including those who identify as secular, from outside.[11] Yet there is much discord. Instead, Hirsi Ali is touted across the globe as a courageous feminist because of her anti-Islamic stance.

In the US, fall 2008, the animated film *Persepolis,* based on Marjane Satrapi's graphic memoirs of her Iranian childhood odyssey, was released. She was nine years old when Shah Pahlavi was deposed and the Islamic revolution changed her life forever. She was exhilarated by the fall of the Shah and his repressive regime, and was confused by the rise of the mullahs who demanded that females wear headscarves. She led a double life after the revolution; outwardly she observed the religious edicts and inwardly she imagined herself free and self-determined. She was twenty-five when she left her family for France to find in the "democratic" West new freedoms from the repressiveness of post-revolutionary Iran. The story is compelling and yet the usual troubling binaries prevail.

Radically plural feminist conversations must take into account the newly forming complexities of today. This complexity develops as the over-used binary secular/religious becomes ever more exhausted and a newer understanding of radical democracy is envisioned. Given the millions of Muslim women in the US, we need to open US political dialogue to their voices. Remember, I am an atheist.

Notes

1   See: Zakia Salime, "The War on Terrorism: Appropriation and Subversion by Moroccan Women", *Signs,* vol. 33, no. 1 (Autumn, 2007), pp. 1–24; Janice C. H. Kim, "The Pacific War and Working Women in Late Colonial Korea", *Signs,* vol. 33, no. 1 (Autumn, 2007), pp. 81–104; and Cawo Moihamed Abdi, "Convergence of Civil War and the Religious Right: Reimagining Somali Women", *Signs,* vol. 33, no. 1 (Autumn, 2007), pp. 183–208.

2   Ayse Gunes-Ayata, "The Politics of Implementing Women's Rights in Turkey", in Jane Boyes and Mayereh Tohidi, eds, *Globalization, Gender and Religion: The Politics of Women's Rights in Catholic and Muslim Contexts* (New York: Palgrave, 2001), pp. 162, 166, 171.

3   Nilufer Gole, *The Forbidden Modern Civilization and Veiling* (Ann Arbor: University of Michigan Press, 1996), pp. 17, 21.

4   Afsaneh Najmabadi, *Women with Mustaches and Men Without Beards* (Berkeley: University of California Press, 2005), pp. 176, 237, 235, 243.

5   Hanna Rosin, "A Boy's Life", *Atlantic Monthly,* vol. 302, no. 4 (November 2009), pp. 56–71.

6   Parvin Pardar, *Women and the Political Process in Twentieth-century Iran* (Cambridge: Cambridge University Press, 1995), pp. 216–218, 219, 220.

7   Hamid eh Sedghi, *Women and Politics in Iran* (London: Cambridge University Press, 2007), pp. 85, 121, 125.

8   Ziba Mir-Hosseini, "Muslim Women's Quest for Equality: Between Islamic Law and Feminism", *Critical Inquiry*, 32 (Summer, 2006), pp. 629, 632. Also see Asma Barlas, *"Believing Women" in Islam* (Austin: University of Texas Press, 2002)

9   Masserat Amir-Ebrahimi, "Blogging from Qom: Behind Walls and Veils", *Comparative Studies of South Asia, Africa and the Middle East*, vol. 28, no 2 (2008), pp. 240, 242, 253.

10 Norma Claire Moruzzi and Fatemeh Sadeghi, "Out of the Frying Pan, Into the Fire: Young Iranian Women Today", *Middle East Report*, 241 (Winter, 2006), pp. 22, 24, 28.

11 Golbarg Bashi, "Women's Rights Gathering, Teheran", June 14, 2006, www.golbargbashi.com/odtoday.html. Also see her: "Shedding Crocodile Tears", www.payvand.com/news/07/mar/ 1062.html and her Ph.D thesis: "Rethinking Human Rights in Iran: A Feminist Perspective" (in process).

22

Heteronormative Silences and Gay Marriage

Even though gay marriage is discussed in present-day politics, the systemic problem of heteronormative privilege—the normalizing and naturalizing of heterosexuality as the standard—is mostly left silent. Individuals are assumed to be heterosexual, and rights are defined legally from this standpoint. Gay marriage unsettles this assumption but does not directly impugn heterosexism as a problem. Although there was much talk about the race and gender of candidates in the 2008 presidential election, their sexual preferences were never identified or queried. It was simply presumed that each candidate was heterosexual.

Bill Clinton brought the rights of gays in the military forth as an issue early on in his administration. Finding little support in 1993 for his position, Clinton caved on the initiative and the notorious policy of "Don't Ask, Don't Tell" went into effect. As such, gays can be in the military so long as they do not reveal their identity, and so long as they act no different than a heterosexual. Females have been welcomed to the military ranks but only if they identify as heterosexual women.

Things have changed a bit. Today—in 2009—three-quarters of Americans think that gays should be able to serve freely in the military. Even Colin Powell now agrees. And it is said that Obama intends to revoke "Don't Ask, Don't Tell".

Still, right-wing advocates in the culture wars put the issue of gay rights center stage. Gay rights remain a passion of the religious right, leading to "religious totalitarianism".[1] For them, gays are godless and undermine all that is moral. Although gay rights have operated as a wedge issue at least since the Reagan era, there is seemingly less success with this strategy today.

Obama meant to temper these past divides with the choice of pastor Rick Warren as the invocation speaker at the 2009 inauguration. Warren identifies gay marriage with pedophilia and incest, and compares abortion to the Nazi Holocaust. Needless to say, gay rights and feminist activists who see Warren as a zealous Christian nationalist did not welcome this choice.

Despite the religious right's zealotry, there have been many electoral victories for gay rights advocates. Gay marriage first became a legal option in the US in Massachusetts and Connecticut. My beloved friend Ellen, mentioned earlier on, who has been at my side for every difficult moment of my adult life, was one of the gay couples along with Maureen, her partner, that initiated the legal request for the right to marry in Massachusetts.

California legalized gay marriage in early 2008. But this right was overturned with the passage of Proposition 8, the same day that California delivered a big election win for Obama. Proposition 8 added fourteen words to the California Constitution declaring that only male–female marriage would be valid and recognized. Opponents of this measure said that this revision is a major change, not simply an amendment, and it therefore needed legislative approval. The California Supreme Court concurred with this reading, Spring 2009.

Many people today say that it is only a matter of time until gay marriage will be a legal right enjoyed throughout the US. The recent legalization of gay marriage in Iowa, in the central "heartland" of the US, in Vermont in April 2009, and in New Hampshire augurs just such change. Vermont's legislature voted to override its governor's veto of gay marriage. Meanwhile for those who wait in other parts of the US, the wait feels too long.

Shortly after Proposition 8 was passed I went to see the movie, *Milk*, about San Francisco gay activist and legend Harvey Milk. Milk was the first gay person to become an elected city official and was killed in 1998 for his aggressive activism. The film documents the hard-fought gay civil rights struggle of the

1970s and 1980s. After viewing the film I was left thinking about how much has changed, and how much has remained the same, in terms of heterosexual privilege.

It is therefore not all that surprising, although it is extremely troubling, to see the tortured and "old" form of heterosexist thinking of the New York State Appeals Court. This court denied the constitutional right to gay marriage to New Yorkers in 2006. A group of the complainants represented in this appeal went forward from Ithaca, New York, my hometown. Richard Stumbar, my spouse, was one of the attorneys who prepared and presented the brief.[2]

New York State's highest Court, in a 4–2 decision, had held that denying marriage to same-sex couples does not undermine equal protection of the law or access to the fundamental right of due process, and therefore does not violate the state constitution. Justice Robert Smith wrote for a plurality of Justices: "We hold that the New York Constitution does not compel recognition of marriages between members of the same sex".[3]

This Appeals Court crafted the question before them as "whether a rational legislature could decide that these benefits should be given to members of opposite-sex couples, but not same-sex couples". This test, commonly known in constitutional jurisprudence as the "rational basis" test, is the lowest level of scrutiny utilized by the courts in judging equal protection claims. In deciding on the constitutionality of laws which burden other groups of individuals with unequal treatment the courts have historically scrutinized the legislation with a more stringent test when the burdened class has had a long history of discriminatory treatment. In not using a heightened standard of review the plurality of the court turned a blind eye to the long history of dis-crimination, hate and violence perpetrated on gays and lesbians.

In applying the rational basis test the plurality of Justices relied on two bases to support the discriminatory classifications in the New York marriage laws. The majority decided that limiting marriage to "a union between a man and a woman" is rational, because heterosexual parents are more suited to raising children than gays or lesbians. However, the record contains support of gay parenting from many prestigious professional groups including psychologists and social workers. The studies show no differences in outcomes between children raised by gays or lesbians and those raised in "traditional" households. Experts be damned, the court had a higher power supporting its decision: "intuition and experience suggest that a child benefits from having before his or her eyes, every day, living models of what a man and a woman are like." An unexamined heteronormativity constructed the court's discriminatory stance.

The Appeals Court majority next relied on the claim that marriage is more necessary for heterosexuals in that they can have unplanned sex and unplanned pregnancies, whereas gays cannot. Marriage is supposed to stabilize this heterosexual whimsy. In the words of the court, "an important function of marriage is to create more stability and permanence in the relationships that cause children to be born". Marriage and "its attendant benefits" become an "inducement", in the words of the court, for opposite-sex couples. As such, marriage is necessitated by the "potential for instability" in heterosexual sexual unions.

The court argued that "homosexuals" plan their pregnancies or adoptions more assiduously and therefore don't need marriage in the same way. "Heterosexual intercourse has a natural tendency to lead to the birth of children; homosexual intercourse does not." Gays "do not become parents as a result of accident or impulse," whereas heterosexuals do. One might assume from this that gays and lesbians are more responsible and careful with their decision making about bearing and rearing children, whereas heterosexuals are more carefree and irresponsible. As such, the law is used to make up for this heterosexual limitation. The court argues why heterosexuals should be included in marriage, rather than arguing why homosexuals should be excluded. However, it is their strengths rather than their limitations that necessitate the exclusion.

The Appeals Court constructed this decision at the lowest level of legal scrutiny using the criterion of rational basis. The Court's decision was to reflect the constitutionality of the laws, and not the morality or immorality of homosexuality. The Court is not supposed to use morality as its criterion for law making and legal decisions. But little else other than heterosexism—given that no factual evidence is provided—can explain the statement that marriage of opposite sexes works better for children than homosexual marriage. No specific data are provided to justify such a claim. The Court clung to its position, writing "that the definition of marriage to include only opposite-sex couples is not irrationally underinclusive".

The Court was reduced to defending its position on the basis of "intuition and experience" that children need to have "living models of what both a man and a woman are like". In the end the people of New York were left with a decision that is poorly written, sloppily argued, and steeped in deep prejudice. We are asked to accept blindly that gay marriage is wrong even though the decision puts forth no plausible rational basis for this claim. If heterosexism is irrational, the decision reads likewise.

Let me unpack the argument a bit further. First I take issue with the strange phrasing that links marriage to opposite sexes. Rather than opposite, males and females form a continuum of biological varieties.[4] And men and women—which are the terms that are used to describe the cultural constructions of what male and female mean—are not one and the same with each other. Male is not synonomous with man, nor female with woman; nor is sex synonymous with gender. The law simply confuses all these subtleties and complexities.

Male and female connote a differentiation of the biological sexes and some scientists like Anne Fausto-Sterling argue that this clear division of two sexes belies the diverse biological realities that sexual identities inhabit, as in inter-sexed individuals. But more to the point here, the construction of gender—of what it means to be a man and a woman—is culturally defined and therefore there are more than two meanings of gender at any given moment. The meaning varies according to time and place and cultural and geographic location. This variety, not surprisingly, applies to the institution of marriage as well.

It makes little sense simply to assert that marriage should be limited to "a union between a man and a woman" or that marriage needs a male and a female. Gender reflects socialization and cultural constructions and meanings. There are many females who choose not to be "women" in a traditional sense of the term, or "womanly" if this means feminine. This is also true for men, and males, and meanings of manhood. So you never exactly know what you are getting when you think you have a man and a woman. No wonder so many heterosexual marriages end in divorce.

According to the law, and human rights norms, marriage is a fundamental right, and according to constitutional jurisprudence, fundamental rights are supposed to be shared by all humans alike. So the Appeals Court had to make gays other-than-human, meaning not like heterosexuals. Their "othering" and differentiating of gays from the normal, even if irresponsible, behavior of heterosexuals are what underpin their decision. There is little use of rational argument, but rather the irrational argument of unexamined heteronormativity formulated as the court's unexamined absolutist moralism.

The equal protection of the law is denied to gays in terms of their right to marry because of prejudice, not reason. If the court had not chosen to view gay marriage as immoral it would have used the criterion of "heightened scrutiny", which would have defined sexual orientation as a "suspect class", like race or gender. With this level of scrutiny gays would have been recognized as a burdened class, and protected with rights as such. Then the long history of discriminatory practices and exclusions and the law that exists to remedy them would have been put in play.

But the Appeals Court not only ignores this history of discrimination, it also confuses gender discrimination with sexual discrimination. So it argues that "limiting marriage to opposite-sex couples" is not engaging in sex discrimination because the "limitation does not put men and women in different classes, and give one class a benefit not given to the other". As such, men and women are treated the same: "They are permitted to marry people of the opposite sex, but not people of their own sex". But by this conflating the categories of sex and gender, gays and lesbians, as such, have no legal standing, and therefore no actionable identity.

Present New York State law that denies gays the right to marry is archaic, uninformed, discriminatory, and exclusionary, much like miscegenation law was in the past. The law in this instance is being read with deep prejudice, and therefore the Court is unable to see its own irrational bias. The Court has chosen to normalize and rationalize its own moral agenda as though it were the same as rational judgment.

Richard is not sure that marriage is worthy of gays, or heterosexuals for that matter. Marriage has varied historically in the US. It was a religious institution before it was orchestrated by the state. It was formerly an institution only applicable to whites; black slaves could not marry. Later, mixed-race marriages were illegal.

At one time the traditional heterosexual family of a man and a woman constituted a clear majority of all marriages. Today, this traditional form defines less than a quarter of all families. More than half of all marriages now end in divorce. Those that remain legally intact often have suffered deceit and the accordant loneliness. What mythology of the family *per se* is the Court protecting here?

Maybe gays are giving up too much of their freedom—their ability to create alternative and meaningful loving unions for themselves and their children—if and when they are allowed to legally marry. Maybe heterosexuals should follow the gay lead here and opt for other family forms. I agree that "marriage is not the only worthy form of family or relationship, nor should it be legally and economically privileged above all others".[5]

Jasbir Puar goes one step further and assesses many of the struggles for gay recognition as forms of "homonationalism"; she concludes that many gains simply create what she terms "placebo rights".[6] Maybe so, but as long as marriage is the legal authorization of people's devotion to each other, gays should have a right to choose it, or not. This is why Richard went before the Court to argue on behalf of twenty-four couples from Ithaca, New York.

How about a gay president, anyone? ... Or, a President who stands behind his campaign promises for full equality and fair treatment of gays.

Notes

1   Michelle Goldberg, *Kingdom Coming* (New York: Norton, 2006), p. 53.
2   Working with Richard were Ithaca attorneys Elizabeth Bixler and Marriette Guildenhys.
3   See the decision of the plurality, written by Justice R. S. Smith, *New York State Reports*, pp. 1, 3, 5, 6, 9, 11, 13, 15.
4   Anne Fausto Sterling, *Sexing the Body* (New York: Basic Books, 2000).
5   See: www.beyondmarriage.org/full_statement.html.
6   See her discussions in Jasbir K. Puar, *Terrorist Assemblages: Homonationalism in Queer Times* (Durham: Duke University Press, 2007).

23

Being White in Cape Town

I traveled to Cape Town with Richard just about three weeks before the presidential election. It was a year to the day since my chemo treatments had ended. I had been asked to discuss "Is the US *Ready* for a Black President?" at Stellenbosch University, South Africa, located an hour and a half outside Cape Town. This university had educated the Afrikaner (white) elite and former presidents during apartheid. The campus—both students and faculty—is still predominantly white. All courses are taught simultaneously in Afrikaans and English.

When I was first asked to address the question of the racial readiness of the US for a black president, my mind flooded with inchoate responses. The question was all the more compelling to me because the people were asking it in Cape Town, home and original site of legal racist apartheid. I also thought it was pretty awful that the question still needed to be asked.

If it were not for the fact that the US has a deep racist history I would not be asked to answer the question at all. It is because being black remains a problem in the States that one imagines this query in the first place. After all, whiteness is not considered a barrier to becoming a US president. Whatever advantage Hillary had at the start derived from her color, obviously, not her gender.

I had several straightforward answers to the initial query I was assigned. African Americans are ready for a black president. Progressives of all colors, including whites, are ready. Young people, on the whole, seem more ready than older people. The US religious right wing isn't ready. White racist men and women are not ready. Dick Cheney and Karl Rove are not ready.

Geraldine Ferraro and other white Hillary supporters are not ready. Yet the globe seems ready. I and all my friends are ready.

I need also to ask whether being ready also means being able. Are US voting booths ready and able? What about the polling sites that newly require photo identification that has disparate racial impact? What of the outdated voter registration rolls in urban and minority areas? What about the impoverished cities with their outdated machines? And what of the two million people in prison who cannot vote, many of whom are black? Or those who have served their prison sentence but still are disenfranchised? And what of the sheer numbers: 94.2 million whites took part in the 2004 election, as compared to 13.5 million blacks?[1]

The US must make itself ready and able. And towards this purpose I revisited much of what happened in the presidential election that pitted race against gender, and gender against race. As a result, race, and with it whiteness and its gender, were deconstructed and then reconstructed creating a post-racial, but not post-racist moment. I also wanted to let my audiences in Cape Town know that more than 90 percent of black women voters in the US had not pulled the lever for Bush/Cheney and should not be blamed.

Most people at Stellenbosch were well versed in the US election and were openly Obama supporters. The audience was predominantly white. Their questions after my talk were animated and energetic. Although my talk critiqued the white privilege of Hillary Clinton's candidacy, and the US more gene-rally, the audience preferred to sidestep this issue. White feminists in South Africa are as slow as many US feminists to recognize and condemn the process when gender parades as white.

Yet a feminist naming of gender seemed even "whiter" for me at Stellenbosch. The racialized silences of gender and feminism appeared starker in a country with a history of racial apartheid. At the end of apartheid in South Africa, some white feminists argued for their inclusion in post-apartheid affirmative action given the patriarchal dimensions of apartheid. I did not agree with this position.

My criticism is not meant to negate the unrelenting burdens of misogyny but to recognize that it operates and is legitimated through white privilege. The only way redress for white women during apartheid makes sense to me is if black women were recognized and recompensed for their double jeopardy—caused by their race and gender—during apartheid. Racial apartheid should make it more difficult to pretend that gender does not have a color.

Maybe gender seems whiter—ensconced in white privilege—in Cape Town because I feel whiter. I am conscious of being white all the time. When I walk along I wonder if any of the white people I am looking at were guilty of grave racial injustice and abuse and torture; whether they were part of the "truth and reconciliation" hearings. In the US, when I was in college, I had worked in the divestment movement to end apartheid. My daughter's first political act was to write a collective letter with her kindergarten class telling Nelson Mandela how happy they were that he had just been released from jail.

All these years later, racial divisions were still starkly drawn in Cape Town. Throughout the city, wherever we walked, we saw white tourists. In the finer neighborhoods we saw only white people. Blacks manned the desks in the hotels, and were the waiters and waitresses in the restaurants. Economic tourism seems to have renewed an economic apartheid that remains racialized.

Things are not the same as before in post-apartheid Cape Town, but they are not different enough. Blacks are more economically successful and therefore differentiated by economic class and its privilege. But the poor are still overwhelmingly black. There is approximately 39 percent unemployment in South Africa. Life expectancy is 43 years for men and 41 for women. The leading causes of death remain AIDS, pneumonia, tuberculosis and influenza. The global economic meltdown along with rising fuel prices have created a sharp increase in food prices and price fixing on bread and milk. Obscene hunger is part of the black landscape. Racial divides exist in all these realities.

While in Cape Town, I also spoke as part of the Public Forum to a mostly black audience at Community House in Salt River, which is a poor middle-class neighborhood. Many radical groups dealing with AIDS, and violence, and prisoners, as well as union and left groups' offices, are housed at Community House. The building was filled with political posters and billboards naming past demonstrations and political demands. Each door inside led to a different office: "Building Women's Activism Campaign" administered by the International Labour Research and Information Group (ILRIG), the sex workers' education taskforce (SWEAT), the victim support for apartheid, the land claims movement, and COSATU (the Congress of South African Trade Unions). The office doors bespoke the difficulties and challenges facing the people of Cape Town. The Public Forum was jointly organized by three non-profits in Community House — Engender, SWEAT and ILRIG.

I was initially sent a title for my talk at the Public Forum at Community House that read: "Capitalist Patriarchy and the Case for Socialist Feminism". This phrasing was actually the title of my first book. Although this title made sense for my thinking almost thirty years ago, it no longer encompassed all that has changed. In the past three decades Marxism and feminism have had a series of changed, or revised dialogues; the Soviet Union collapsed; China embraced capitalism, as has the globe itself; many new feminisms developed; socialism and feminism, as terms, became as problematic as they are helpful. Given all this, I needed a different title.

I offered a new title, hesitantly because I was trying to stay within the interests expressed by the first title that was chosen. My newer title was *Global Obscenities and New Anti-imperial Feminisms*. I thought, this at least makes clear that capitalism is now a global systemic problem and that there are many forms of anti-capitalist/anti-empire feminist stances today, some of which might be called socialist. But I still wondered if the term "socialism" would be helpful. It is usually not so in the US, but maybe it would have more resonance in Cape Town.

Bernadette Muthien, my wonderful host and director of Engender—a group dedicated to thinking beyond binary sex and gender divides—asked if I might change the title to: *Feminist Anti-Imperialism*. She and the co-organizers of the Public Forum were concerned that my title and talk should be as accessible as possible, since many grassroots community members would attend. I responded that of course this title could work. For me, a title for a talk is an invitation to others who might want to think along with you. If this was what they wanted to think about, I would use it as my starting point.

My one hesitation is that "anti-imperialism" assumes that imperialism is the framework; that there still is a demarcated center and a periphery to the globe; that there are countries that are the exploiters and others that are exploited; that there still are stark borders and boundaries around nations. None of these realities are true the way they once were. Although exploitation continues and countries are occupied, and colonized, it is often not perfectly clear how the more porous relations of the globe create the newest complexities of power.

Similarly, feminisms exist in both imperial and exploited countries, and in all variety of kinds. Many women across the globe adopt feminism but in imperial form. Others stand against capitalist exploitation in its particularly misogynist and racist forms. Others merge the lines. It is to this new complexity that I wanted to speak and think with the people at the Community House. I wanted to explore how feminisms today are both a great promissory against global capitalism in its racialized patriarchal forms and also a decoy system for the new global obscenities of excessive inequality and poverty.

I also wanted to take this particular historical moment—the

US 2008 presidential election—and say how important it is to always be ready to think newly and how hard this is to do. And that despite the hopefulness of this moment there is also despair across the globe given the new horrors of global capitalism. Yet progressives across the world must drag their radical commitments with them as we search for new political possibilities.

I was deeply moved to be having this discussion in South Africa with people who have suffered so much already. I thought back to my earliest political work on economic divestment from South Africa. And was also reminded that Obama remembers, too, his early political activism in college when he was committed to South African divestment.[2]

Richard and I hiked Table Mountain that sits almost in the middle of the city. From the trails that line the mountain, we had gorgeous vistas of the deep blue and green ocean. Some days the mountain is covered in clouds. The beauty of the city sits uncomfortably as a backdrop to the townships that meander outwards from the city. The shanties speak an unforgiving poverty without potable water or plumbing. Inside the city almost everyone speaks about the violence and crime. There is much fear. The almost-all white rich neighborhoods are built like fortresses with barbed wire, electric fences, high cement walls, and steel barricades.

I know that we have incredibly unfair riches in the US and gated communities that are also enclaves of white privilege. Yet, I wonder if this newest economic apartheid in Cape Town is also not a specific racist legacy of the apartheid era. Some political activists offer their own understanding of what exists today: a new apartheid with black managers.

These queries about the lingering presence of white privilege in Cape Town, or Zimbabwe, keep recurring. Mahmood Mamdani writes that Zimbabwe suffers not simply from Mugabe's corrupt rule, but from the complex struggles over the white control of land in postcolonial African countries. Recognition of current crises in Zimbabwe must be set within the context of these struggles by victims of settler colonialism, and the effects of structural adjustment, alongside several major droughts, due in part to global warming, that create untold suffering.[3] South Africa is suffering in like ways, without a Mugabe.

On another day Richard and I hike up through the Bo Kaap neighborhood where slaves from the Dutch East Indies were originally housed during colonialism. The houses are all painted in bright colors and a rainbow of energy speaks of the Muslim community housed here. We visit the small local museum that documents the slave trade. And we walk along the pathways of a local school where children are making their happy noises in the playground.

Richard, as an attorney in the US, keeps wondering with me how South Africa can have the most progressive constitution in the world, disallowing all and any form of discrimination, and still have such glaring inequalities. Even gays have full rights in South Africa, including civil unions that are often considered more progressive than traditional marriage. We both wonder when their constitution will become more than words.

While in Cape Town I continually am reminded that change is very slow, and yet the changes matter deeply. While I was still there the ANC (African National Congress) was hemorraghing. The Zuma-led ANC has dismissed President Mbeki, and a neoliberal group had splintered from the ANC and formed their own political party. Our cab driver said that none of the politicians care about the people. He yearned for another Mandela but said there was none in sight.

When I was on chemo my friend Peyi Airewele Soyinka taught me how to wrap my head in scarves, Nigerian style. Maybe seeing so many head wraps forged my deep sense of connect while in Cape Town. The moon was full. The wind at Cape Point was fierce and invigorating. The foods of the world—Iraqi, Moroccan, Indian, and Afghan—were incredibly sensuous. The tastes were intense. It was spring, with flowers coming into bloom. I made myself feel hopeful that change would be coming.

At the time, I wondered if maybe there would be a landslide victory for Barack and the voting lines would wrap around for miles, like in the beginning of post-apartheid South Africa. Then, millions of blacks turned out for their first time to vote defiantly and hopefully for Mandela. Maybe it would be first-time voters in the US, as well, to make a new electoral map as "America becomes more tolerant, and not to put too fine a point on it, less white."[4] I could hope. And I did, as we left Cape Town for home.

Notes

1   Andrew Hacker, "Obama: The Price of Being Black", *New York Review of Books*, vol. LV, no. 15 (September 25, 2008), pp. 12, 13.
2   Barack Obama, *Dreams From My Father* (New York: Three Rivers Press, 1995).
3   Mahmood Mamdani, "Lessons of Zimbabwe" *London Review of Books*, December 4, 2008, at www.portside.org.
4   Paul Krugman, "A Fateful Election", *New York Review of Books*, vol. LV, no. 17 (November 6, 2008), p. 13.

24

On the Ground in Florida

I am waiting on the tarmac in the Philadelphia airport on my way to Miami. It is October 31, 2008, Halloween, four days before the presidential election. I will meet Rebecca who has already been there for more than a week. She was trained earlier on to be a deputy field officer tasked with training volunteers in the campaign. She is my extraordinary friend and roommate from college days who has been deeply involved in the Obama campaign from the start. You may remember I mentioned earlier that she slept in my hospital room during my surgery and sat by my side for my last chemo infusion.

While waiting for the plane to take off I remembered the last time I had been to Miami. I was in college and Rebecca and I went down to visit my Aunt Nettie during our spring break. It was 1968 and Miami was very white then. When I arrived this time I saw a multiethnic, multiracial diversity in the airport, and in the neighborhoods as I entered the city. I thought to myself, if this is Florida, Barack can win.

Rebecca was the Director of Special Grants for the MacArthur Foundation in 1985 when they helped fund Barack Obama through the Developing Communities Project (DCP) that focused on the South Side of Chicago. The closing of the steel mills had devastated this area. Barack had just returned to Chicago after finishing law school and was about twenty-four years old at the time. This started his community organizing days that we have heard so much about. He organized in 2000 a huge voter registration drive, called Project Vote, and registered 150,000 new African American voters in Chicago in that year. Rebecca knew his talents and was deeply committed to bringing them to the national stage. She brought me along with her.

When I left for Miami, Florida was considered very much up for grabs. Obama had just about a three-point lead in the polls against McCain. Two nights before I left Barack aired his multi-million-dollar infomercial. He voiced the stories of struggling families with their punishing lives—with the stresses of low-paying jobs, exorbitant healthcare costs, and fears of bankruptcy. It was Obama at his best: asking us to hope and find our better selves.

Meanwhile McCain and Palin were making their last-ditch effort—after the "inexperience" and "terrorist" labels failed to make headway for them—to smear Obama as a socialist, as someone who would redistribute the wealth. Obama responded easily and in relaxed fashion. He says we need to share more, and if sharing his toys in kindergarten makes him a socialist, so be it. I wondered if the ideals of socialism, spoken in terms of sharing with and caring for others, might be salvaged out of all this acrimony.

Bill Clinton and Barack had just done a rally together in Gainesville the night before I arrived. Al and Tipper Gore were stumping for Obama throughout the state. Hillary had been in Florida earlier in the week. Obviously, it would be great for Barack to win here especially given Florida's role in the defeat of Gore in 2000. By the time I arrived, hundreds of thousands of Floridians—waiting on lines for up to five hours—had already successfully voted during early voting days. I was getting very eager to get to the Obama Liberty City office headquarters to become a part of all this campaign energy.

Liberty City is a poor neighborhood. On many streets there are abandoned houses and signs of inner-city decay. Most houses are barricaded against potential theft and violence. But amidst this urban blight there are also simple homes neatly groomed. The neighborhood reminded me of canvassing in north Philadelphia during the primaries where many of the row houses were abandoned and yet children happily played in the streets.

The Liberty City streets were a mix of creative resilience and punishing poverty. There were many Obama signs proudly in view.

Wherever I visit in Liberty City I see steel gratings over windows and protective screens to deter assailants. There is only fast food to be found anywhere close by. When we went to fill the car with gas at the local station there was no easy outside credit card service. We had to pay in advance, and if you are using a credit card you have to prove your identity first. Everything reminds you that if you live in these neighborhoods you are not trusted. And yet our office is located in a newly renovated shopping center that speaks the pride of the neighborhood.

The day I arrived Rebecca introduced me to Karen Andre who is the field organizer for the Liberty City office. She is a 30-year-old young Haitian-American attorney. She is responsible for too much and nothing lessens this overload. Yet the volunteers surround her with their enthusiasm, their grit, and their energy. Everyone is determined to make an Obama victory happen. There are new people trickling in and out of the office eager to help, and there are also people who return each day for long stretches at a time. There are also a few hustlers who want Obama signs or other gear, possibly to sell, but Karen navigates this all with skill and sensitivity. She is a part of this community and she holds it to its best commitments.

I next met lovely Mary and DC, who are from Chicago and Santa Cruz, and are also Rebecca's friends, and white like the two of us. I am conscious of the white privilege that distinguishes the four of us and makes it "special" that we chose to come to Miami to work on behalf of Obama. This makes me more self-conscious than I might otherwise have been about the particular role white women have played in our country's racist past. So I think about this racial divide, but I do not feel uncomfortable. I am just conscious of knowing my black co-workers have a right to their own skepticism about me, or any of us four white women, though none is openly shown.

Geraldine Kilpatrick Owens, better known as Ms. or Mama Gerri, oversees the daily practices of the Liberty City office. She cooks great lemon pies and strawberry cakes for the volunteers and staff. She is on chemotherapy for incurable cancer and she tells me that she has made a promise to work for her community in the time she has left. She deeply wants Barack to win and says she will do everything she can to make this happen. Gerri, like most of the other Obama volunteers, is deeply spiritual and sees Barack's run for president in this light.

Vicki Augustus-Fidelia says: for Barack, I will do anything needed—even though her joints ache with arthritis. Carolyn, who is in her late sixties and on dialysis, says, as she gets up to stretch her creaky body, she is making history by volunteering. Mostly everyone making phone calls begins their call identifying themselves as part of the Obama campaign for change. And they end with "God bless" or "Have a blessed day". Though I am not religious their religiosity did not seem troubling to me. They were not exclusionary or proselytizing.

The first day I was in the office the canvassers knocked on 2,864 doors. The Liberty City office had the most knocks in all of Florida on that day. I wondered whether these knocks would matter enough. Would enough people continue to turn out, especially on election day, for Barack to win?

Other than the locals, volunteers came from all over. Six young white male students from the University of Copenhagen in Denmark were at the Liberty City office for two weeks. They had contacted the national Obama headquarters more than a year in advance to plan their trip. They were at the ready for whatever was requested of them. I asked them why they had come to work on an election so far from home. They said that the world is so interconnected today that it matters to them who is president here. They were tired of Bush/Cheney and the lawlessness of the US. They think that global warming must be addressed. They see the melting ice and think something must be done. They say they come from a small country with little global power, but think they can make a small difference by helping Obama get elected.

There were also the six fabulous young black women whom I so enjoyed getting to know: Traci, Janel, Sabrina, Samarria, Janay and Rebecca, from Texas, Tennessee, Georgia, Alabama and Florida. They are longtime friends. Black professionals. It was a girlfriend thing. They knew they had to do something: they were "witnessing for Obama". They said they were from states where McCain was sure to win, so they came to Florida to do something that might count. They were filled with energy and friendship and hard work and they were in Florida to make a difference that mattered.

On my second day in the office everyone got excited when Spike Lee visited and shook his or her hands. The next day Karen took me to Little Haiti for a pro-Obama rally. The rally took place across the street from the Lemon City Public Library where long lines of early voters were already waiting to vote. The line had started forming at 6:00 a.m. The speakers and performers at the rally helped the time pass more quickly. The rally speakers kept reminding those waiting to vote and those in the crowd that no one should make them think that they cannot vote. Demand the information you need. Do not be intimidated. Demand your rights. All the rally speakers addressed the crowd in both English and Creole. Paul Farmer, the well-known doctor and AIDS activist who has set up clinics in Haiti, spoke to the crowd about affordable health care.

This rally was something more than election politics. It reflects a movement that goes beyond the election. The signs scattered throughout the crowd were in Creole: Chanjman Nou Bezwen/Change We Can Believe In. One speaker tells the crowd that 99 percent of Haitians are for Obama. They hope he will change US policy towards Haiti. But she follows up saying that their work only starts with Obama's victory on Tuesday. They chant: No more trickle down—we want bottom up. The astounding energy of Little Haiti in Miami felt truly promissory.

As I stood in the crowd, I was thinking that I could just as easily be in Haiti, or Cape Town. But, happily, this was also America.

On Sunday and Monday I am asked to oversee the phone banking. I give out the cell phones and the call lists and the talking sheets. It is noisy. There are no windows in our phone room. I am amazed at the constancy of those making the calls to get people out to vote. There are such strong feelings of hope.

Food is donated daily for the volunteers by several of the local restaurants. People appreciate the meals and the camaraderie. I am getting to know the women I am working with. I am learning Florida election law so I can answer questions from felons and new voters. A few felons are automatically restored to the voting rolls but most must follow cumbersome and arduous steps to be reinstated. One 18-year-old called and said he was turned away when he tried to vote because he just had his school identification card. I told him to go back to the poll with his father and find a poll watcher, because he had what he needed in order to vote. He called me back after casting his vote, ecstatic with his victory. Just one day to go.

It is finally November 4, the day of reckoning. Rebecca and Mary and I head to the office early. DC had promised to be home for the night of the election and had already left for California. Everyone is filled with anticipation. The phone bankers are once again told that each and every vote counts. The office is noisy and busy. Canvassers are deployed in three shifts. Cars are sent out to bring to the polls the last people that still need rides. There are more volunteers than we can actually use. On the ground, activism is reaching a peak. But because of two weeks of early voting there are not the long lines that were feared on this last day. Things are moving smoothly but with great excitement and wonderment.

Election day is coming to a close. The last phone calls are made. I go out with Rebecca for a final round of knocking on doors to flush out anyone who might not have voted yet. We find that most everyone has already voted. In fifteen minutes the polls will close and voting will end. When we get back to the Liberty City office the phone banking room is emptied of its people. Our office has knocked on 7,000 doors and made even more phone calls.

Balloons are blown up in anticipation of a celebration. Office workers are starting to move tables and spread out the food — nachos, burritos, chicken wings, pizza, and so on. A big screen has been connected to a computer so all of us can listen to and watch the voting returns together. Horns are beginning to honk loudly in the street outside our office. Loud music began to fill the air. A boisterous party in the streets is taking form.

There is an overwhelming sense that all the work has mattered; that people are deeply moved that they have made a difference; that much is possible when people unite together. The activism and commitments of this campaign have created a mobilized community in Liberty City, and in thousands of like places across the country. This sense of affirmation was felt by millions of people who had chosen to partake. And this was before anyone knew if Barack had won.

We start to gather with one another around the big screen. Karen calls us together for the moment. She tells everyone that she will not thank them for what they have done, but rather congratulate them on what they have done. She individually recognizes everyone's work, and we all rejoice. And then the returns start to come in.

Vermont goes for Obama. And then Pennsylvania too. People seem to start to let themselves believe that Barack is going to win. There are wild screams of joy. More states are declared Obama's. And then he finally does the unbelievable. Obama wins. Much later into the night, he wins Florida. Rebecca and I were so tired, but not too tired to love the fact that Florida was turned blue.

Watching the joy of Barack's win was electrifying. I loved seeing the hundreds of thousands of people in Chicago's Grant Park; and the tens of thousands in Harlem; and the young women of Spelman College rejoice in the streets. There was an extraordinary joy in the air, an amazing outpouring of hopefulness and expectation and affirmation. It was glorious that we had finally said, as Americans, that things must change. Millions of Americans had said no to Bush/McCain and yes to Obama. It is a longed-for break with the past, even if unknown in detail.

As I go through the security line at Miami airport on my way home to Ithaca not one person around me is speaking English. All I hear are the many voices and languages of this country. Surprisingly, my plane actually takes off on time. As I wait in the Philadelphia airport for my delayed plane to Ithaca, I am very tired but very happy. Something has happened.

What Is Next?

Unfinished Beginnings and Endings

I started writing this frame two days after Obama won the election. I continued my writing through to three months after the inauguration. The economic downturn has worsened and the complications with Iraq, Afghanistan, and Pakistan are deeply troubling. I am already feeling and sounding less hopeful than I did at the start.

Nevertheless, I continue to grab hold of my early sense of relief if not a bit of joy that the "wicked demagogue—I will not use 'witch'—of the West" had been unseated. It felt like a regime change maybe not so unlike the demise of the dictatorship of Pinochet in Chile, or the end of the German occupation of Poland during World War Two, or the fall of the Berlin Wall in 1989.[1] The rogue era of Bush/Cheney's lawlessness and unconscionable greed had, I hoped, come to an end.

The Bush/Cheney regime was our Stalin and it was time for us to recognize that its version of privatized capitalism and its thuggery were way too egregious to be salvageable. Sure, there are huge differences expressed in the events I mention, and maybe at best it is a US palace coup, but how else to explain the throngs of ecstatic people in Harlem, Atlanta, and Chicago, and the dancing in the streets in Kenya, and elsewhere across the globe?

I will say again that I am relieved that Bush and Cheney are out of the White House and McCain and Palin did not get to enter it. Early on there was a sense of new possibility both here and abroad because of this. The world has embraced Obama's victory as a good sign. Many countries in the Middle East are hesitant to celebrate fully, but they also think that Obama may be a change for the better. Iraqi officials feel more hopeful about a timed schedule for US troop withdrawal that Obama will abide by.

I continue to hope that Obama's victory is the righteous response to US despair and desperate shame about Guantánamo, and Katrina, and Iraq. And that the early jubilation and celebration have given way to vigilant committment to a newly radicalized, democratic democracy. Progressives of all stripes — civil rights and gay activists, anti-racist feminists, environ-mentalists, health advocates, economic justice workers — must engage their joy in order to stay focused on and organized around a radically democratic agenda.

Barack will, I hope, be instrumental in allowing for the big changes that are needed, but as June Jordan in her "Poem for South African Women" wrote as they fought against apartheid: "We are the ones we have been waiting for".[2] But I am getting ahead of myself here.

Post-election, Palestinians and progressive Jews were disappointed with the choice of Rahm Emmanuel, who has a record as a hawkish Zionist, for Chief of Staff, but remain cautiously optimistic about Obama's diplomatic overtures toward the Muslim world. It is also true that the more recent horrors done to Palestinians in Gaza make any sense of optimism hard to sustain.

On the other hand, in New Zealand, Maoris, an indigenous group that has faced much discrimination, said post-election that they have new hope that they too may find justice, like some African Americans in the US. Ahmadinejad early on sent a letter of congratulation to Obama from Iran. This unclear sense of an embrace of newness, even if not easily defined, means something. It is not "nothing" that has happened with the 2008 election.

And yet there were also early warning signs, which remain at issue, that much is left unresolved for a progressive agenda. California, the same state that made a huge difference for Obama in the popular vote and his victory, chose to deny full civil rights for gay people by voting for Proposition 8, a constitutional amendment that bans gay marriage. Black and Latinas were largely held accountable for this anti-gay result with many of them identifying their religious beliefs as their reason. This rollback of marriage rights for gays dampened the election euphoria for many. Obama's victory felt less deep and less thick as a victory for civil and human rights because of it. However, the defeat was narrow and not robust: just 51 percent for Prop. 8, and 49 against. Many say that gay marriage rights will happen, in time, and soon.

Post-election euphoria is passing, but hope is still in the air. In the early days after the election my mind pulled me toward the positive, over and over again. Reproductive rights were enthusiastically endorsed on November 4. The right-to-life referendum in Colorado went down to a whopping defeat, with 73 percent of voters rejecting amending the state's constitution to give rights to fertilized eggs. Personhood was rejected as beginning at conception. Voters in California once again turned back the attempt to mandate parental notification in the case of minors having abortions. Similar pro-abortion forces won in South Dakota, saying no to an abortion ban that would have allowed the procedure only for rape, incest and grave risk to the life of the mother. This is all to the good.

Women of all colors elected Obama. They turned out in large numbers, making up 53 percent of the voters, with 56 percent of us voting for Barack. Women voted in greater numbers than men—who were 47 percent of the voters and 49 percent of his vote. This created a significant gender gap ranging from seven to thirteen points, depending on the state. So women of the rainbow were electorally formidable. They need to remain formidable in order to keep the focus on the sexual, gender, and racial needs of all people for global peace, economic justice, and environmental health.

An open letter written on December 16, 2008 by many of the leaders of established US mainstream women's groups asked for a cabinet-level Office on Women to insure the needed and appropriate focus on women's issues and needs. As a result, this initiative was begun. Meanwhile much remains to be resolved — both inside and outside electoral politics and the newly formed in-between spaces of this political moment.

As the almost $800 billion economic stimulus package evolved, national women's rights advocacy groups entered the fray, with some effect. The initial stimulus package focused on rebuilding the economic infrastructure — bridge building, road repair, and so on — with little mention of the social infrastructure jobs that define opportunities for wage-earning women. The latest version of the package focused on "investments in health care, education, and job training". According to Lindsay Beyerstein, these "expenditures are expected to create or sustain significant numbers of jobs in female-dominated sectors of the economy, like teaching, nursing, and social work".[3]

Women, along with some men, also need childcare and day-care facilities; they need assist in higher education; they need help with the care-giving domains of society. With a majority of single-parent families headed by women, and a majority of married women in the labor force, the economy cannot recover without "stimulating" both the familial and public realms of labor.[4] The particular racialized gender burdens and locations of women must continue to be uncovered. Women of all colors need, what I have elsewhere called "polyversal" recognition if the difficulties of their lives and their families are to be adequately addressed.[5]

Time continues to pass. Valerie Jarrett, a single mother and close friend of the Obamas from their days of Chicago politics, was co-chair for the Obama transition team. She promised to the US public accountability, visibility, and diversity of all sorts and kinds. She has inclusiveness in the way she thinks and speaks. She said that the Obama team would hit the ground running. His cabinet appointments rolled out a new rainbow of colors that was also considerably female. This all looked potentially significant and important.

But there was also reticence and disappointment that so many of Obama's economic team were Clinton retreads, and that Hillary would be Secretary of State. Some of the new was already looking very old. The press needled Obama about Clinton's appointment and her former hawkish foreign policy stance. He denied that there was a problem between them, and said that they share a worldview. He assured us that he is the one in charge; the one with the vision; the one who will make this be differently new.

I was more than a little uncomfortable with Obama's explanation of what he was doing. I wondered about his individualistic standpoint. After all, his vision is not his alone; nor can his victory be won in singular fashion. Barack's win comes from decades of civil and gay rights and anti-war and feminist struggles. His notion of coalition building is indebted to that of Martin Luther King's early work and Jesse Jackson's Rainbow Coalition. The on-the-ground organizing of the Obama campaign utilized longtime established community networks in neighborhoods throughout the USA.[6] He is not carved out of his own whole cloth, and even though he says he knows this, I am not sure he fully understands this.

Time is still passing. The economy continues to jolt back and forth. There are more lay-offs. This day it is the delivery service DHL in Ohio that is closing down. Three women are interviewed on CBS TV news and cry. They say that their lives are ruined and the futures of their families are destroyed. I carry their sobs with me through the day.

Later in the same day I go to the Africana Center at Cornell University to hear Patricia McFadden speak about feminisms in Zimbabwe. She wants the US out of Africa. Although she thinks Barack is "a perfect human being" she also believes that he will rule in the interests of a class that are not in the interests of most of Africa. She is filled with humanity but fears that Obama will obfuscate the struggle that must happen for full justice to define the globe. She likens Obama to Nelson Mandela, but not in a positive way. She thinks Mandela, in the end, softened the struggle against white supremacy too much.[7] That he made life too comfortable for whites in the new South Africa. I leave the discussion, troubled, and wondering about what lies ahead.

The worry is only heightened the next day when Obama chooses pastor Rick Warren to open the inauguration. I do not accept that Rick Warren and his exclusionary religious views should be part of an inaugural message. If Obama is reaching for a new inclusivity let him choose a progressive Buddhist monk, or a rabbi, or an imam. I think that Obama should be more cautious how he chooses to embrace religiosity in the US if the embrace is not to endorse the very punishing radicalism that we war against elsewhere.

Finally inauguration day comes and the country and the globe celebrate together despite the complex surround. There is utter joy in our streets. The Washington Mall is covered with millions of exuberant and incredulous faces. The music, the poetry, the words of this day are to be cherished. I deeply feel and celebrate the total and complete happiness and miraculousness of this day. Whatever it is not, Barack and Michelle and their two girls as a black family form a new imaginary for the US.

In very short order Barack starts governing. He announces the reversal of the existing ban on stem cell research, and proposes new climate rules that will protect the environment and put limits on carbon dioxide emissions. He ends the gag rule that monitors international aid according to whether abortion is allowed in the would-be-recipient country or not. He commits to closing Guantánamo detention center within the year. He appoints special envoys to the Middle East and Afghanistan. He extends medical coverage to 4 million poor children in the US. This all feels truly different.

He speaks to the Muslim world directly on Arab TV and extends a willing hand. But then he continues to authorize the use of drone-delivered bombs in Pakistan. And he assigns 17,000 more US troops, and then an additional 4,000, by late March, to

Afghanistan. Obama spoke during the election of re-directing US attention towards Afghanistan. I am totally opposed to this militarist option. His stance undermines the possibility for new progressive opportunities for the globe.

Yet I am not ready for closure. It feels important to imagine that America might be other than what it has been, even if it has not yet become exactly what I wish for. There has been a shift from the discourse of state terrorism and unilateralist bludgeoning toward negotiation and multilateralism that has still not been fully played out. The economic bailouts and stimulus packages remain too protective of the crooks, but the need for oversight and economic regulation is in play. Small incremental steps are insufficient and worrisome because the problems are so big. Yet I tell myself that radical democrats must remain in these uncomfortable spaces demanding the different world that we wish for.

My thoughts are a mix of optimism and pessimism. On a bad day I think back to the earliest euphoria and use this energy to try and think like a hopeful radically democratic democrat, still. To remind myself of ending the war in Iraq while not mobilizing one in Afghanistan and Pakistan; resolving the crisis in Gaza and the Middle East; creating universal and affordable health care; rebuilding the economic and social infrastructure with jobs and available day care; developing energy alternatives; creating alternatives to global warming; insuring an end to hunger and homelessness; creating full civil rights for each and every human being; guaranteeing a living wage for each person with no person ever amassing excessive wealth over another; enforcing justice for Palestinians; creating full access to one's reproductive rights; ending the military/armaments lobby; curbing agribusiness and reclaiming the earth; establishing accessible and good universal education for all; freeing humanity from violence and torture and war; creating talk and negotiation with Sudan, Korea, China, Rwanda, Iran; and ending the manufacturing of new enemies.

I keep reminding myself that radically democratic anti-racist feminists are needed. A renewed activism must be achieved through this negotiation with the do-able and un-doable; the practical and the dream; the inside and the outside; the reform and the revolutionary; the disciplined and the uncontrollable. None of these divides exist as they once were because there are newly new configurations of power—along sex, gender, race and class lines—that must be utilized with new effect. Do not pigeonhole my thinking or yours or Obama's at this moment.

I am not a s/hero worshipper. Worship worries me. Instead, I value what ordinary folks can do together when we care about each other and the world we inhabit. Obama may no longer be the ordinary person he once was. (He spent close to three quarters of a billion dollars to become president.) But maybe he can effectively be reminded. I still want to believe that he wants to be reminded.

It is ordinary folk who must keep the everyday needs of all people at center stage. It is from and with this vision that the rainbow of "newest" democracies will unfold. This unfolding must unhinge and unmoor the existing constraints on our sexual, gendered, raced, and classed imaginings.

Let me return to my start, of sorts, in this political moment, before finishing. I spoke at a pro-Obama rally in Ithaca, New York, at the State Theatre on February 1, 2008. I said: "We need to make sure that Barack is elected and then we must take our outrage at our defunct democracy and create an activated, engaged, radical, insistent electorate demanding democracy for everyone at home and abroad. We can settle for nothing less. Yes we can. We must. And we will."

We, the big "we" that I have written about in earlier moments, must create a politics of and for the globe that we have not quite figured out yet. The election of Obama is most probably not sufficient for the radical change needed. His election may rather simply be the proof that things can change and need to continue to do so. We must keep looking for the new configurations of power in order to create newer ones that will allow the planet's humanity to thrive.

Whatever has happened by the time you read this, and however many mistakes have been made, despondency is disallowed. Despondency and passivity are options the globe cannot afford. It still remains, in June Jordan's words, that "we are the ones that we have been waiting for". The change we wish for will crystallize as the full consequences of this moment are unveiled and then resisted and recrafted. And although the change we hope for has not fully happened yet, it has begun.

Notes

1 Darryl Pinckney had similar thoughts. See his comment in his "Obama: In the Irony-Free Zone", *New York Review of Books*, vol. LV, no. 12 (December 18, 2008), p. 18.

2 June Jordan, "Poem for South African Women", *Passion: New Poems, 1977–1980* (Boston: Beacon Press, 1980), p. 42.

3 Lindsay Beyerstein, "Women's Groups See Success in Stimulus", *Washington Independent*, January 29, 2009, and at: http://washingtonindependent.com/27846/women-and-the-stimulus.

4 Randy Albelda, "The Macho Stimulus Plan", *Boston Globe*, www.bostonglobe.com, November 28, 2008.

5 See my *Against Empire*, Chapter 8 (London: Zed Books, 2004).

6 Paul Ortiz, "On the Shoulders of Giants: Senator Obama and the Future of American Politics", *truthout/perspective*, November 25, 2008, www.truthout.org/112508R.

7 Patricia McFadden, "Resisting Neo-liberalism: Struggles for Lives of Dignity and Peace", paper delivered at the Women and Gender Studies Symposium, Syracuse University, November, 2008. Also see her "Issues of Gender and Development from an African Feminist Perspective", lecture at the Center for Gender and Development Studies, University of the West Indies, Bridgetown, Barbados, November, 2000.

Index